THE MOVIE MAKING BOOK

SKILLS & PROJECTS
TO LEARN & SHARE

This book is dedicated to every single young movie maker that has taken part in the last six years of Sparks workshops, holiday projects and birthday parties. Your creativity has inspired us!

Frances Lincoln Limited
A subsidiary of Quarto Publishing Group UK
74–77 White Lion Street
London N1 9PF

The Movie Making Book
Copyright © Frances Lincoln 2017
Text copyright © Dan Farrell & Donna Bamford
Photographs copyright © Dan Farrell & Donna Bamford
except for 7, 11 (bottom), 13 (top), 19 (bottom), 21, 23, 63, 110, 111, 113, 115, 117 (bottom 2), 132, 133 (top) © Sheena Holliday, 38 © Axstokes/Shutterstock, 39 © Pavel L Photo and Video/Shutterstock, 47 (bottom) © Denis Kuvaev/Shutterstock, 83 (middle left) © Claudia Paulussen/Shutterstock, 83 (top) © Bildagentur Zoonar GmbH/Shutterstock, 83 (right) © Steve Mann/Shutterstock, 83 (bottom) © cynoclub/Shutterstock, 85 © Africa Studio/Shutterstock, 89 (left) © Kati Molin /Shutterstock, 89 (right) © Africa Studio/Shutterstock, 94 © ESB Professional/Shutterstock, 109 © bikeriderlondon/Shutterstock, 135 (right) © Alexander Kazantsev/Shutterstock.

Interior illustrations: Camcorder © Keep Calm and Vector/Shutterstock, Character profile © Epifantsev/Shutterstock, Camera on tripod © VectorsMarket/Shutterstock, Pencil © sivVector/Shutterstock, Pencil & storyboard © Honza Hruby/Shutterstock, Computer © Keep Calm and Vector/Shutterstock, Microphone © Keep Calm and Vector/Shutterstock, Present © Keep Calm and Vector/Shutterstock, Smartphone © Keep Calm and Vector/Shutterstock, Cat © Keep Calm and Vector/Shutterstock.

A catalogue record for this book is available from the British Library.

ISBN 978-0-7112-3887-9

Printed and bound in China

9 8 7 6 5 4 3 2 1

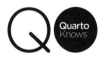

Quarto is the authority on a wide range of topics.

Quarto educates, entertains and enriches the lives of our readers – enthusiasts and lovers of hands-on living.

www.QuartoKnows.com

THE MOVIE MAKING BOOK

SKILLS & PROJECTS
TO LEARN & SHARE

DAN FARRELL
& DONNA BAMFORD

F
FRANCES
LINCOLN

CONTENTS

GETTING STARTED

One of the most important things to know about movie making is that movies are made up of lots of individual shots, just like a sentence is made up of lots of words, or a wall is built out of lots of bricks. Movie makers put one shot next to another, and another, in a sequence that they use to tell stories to an audience.

In the first part of this book, you'll find lots of projects that will help you to master different shots and storytelling techniques. Each project is designed to offer you the tools to become an accomplished movie maker at home. They cover different areas linked to making movies – from camera skills to script writing, special effects and more – and get more complex as you go through. You can follow through the projects one by one, or dip in and out as you choose.

Later on in the book, you'll find longer projects where you can apply all your new skills and take your movie making to the next level. The projects are all suitable for movie makers aged seven and upwards, although some may require help from adults. To extend your movie-making skills, follow our Pro Tips to help you get professional-looking results.

In doing these projects, you'll be able to create movies to share with your family and friends. The final part of the book gives you helpful advice for publishing your films, including ways to stay safe online. You can even share them with other movie-makers on our special channel, or host your own movie premieres. Soon, you'll have your own collection of movies to celebrate.

Happy Movie Making!

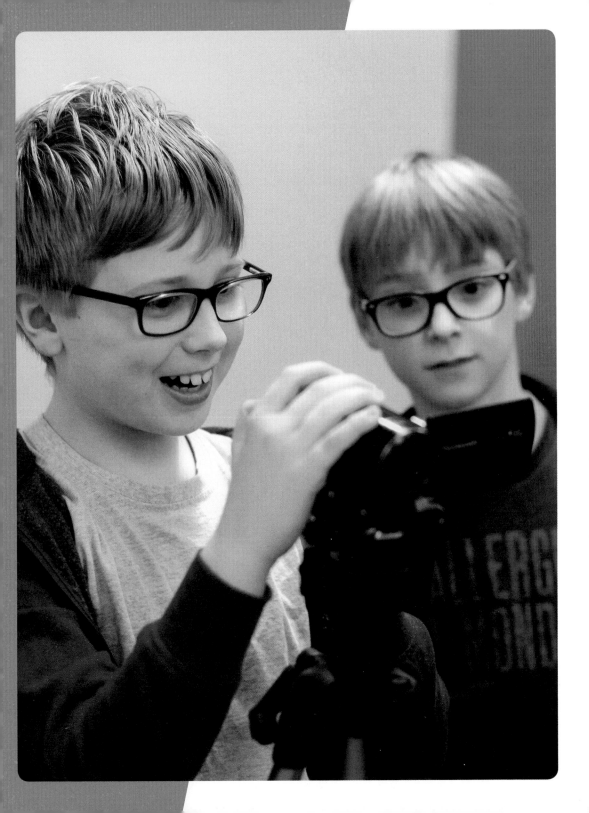

MOVIE
SHOTS

In this section of the book, there are lots of short projects that will help you to master your skills and knowledge of shots as a movie maker.

The projects will introduce you to specific tools used by professional movie makers. In each project, we've recommended some example shots to get you started, but you can use any of these skills in your own movies too.

Each shot has a particular purpose and can be used to great effect in your movie making. Try experimenting with each of the shot types to build up your skills, ready to apply them to the follow-on movie-making projects and your own movies too.

For these projects, you'll need some basic camera equipment, such as a phone or tablet camera, or a camcorder. Take a look at our Equipment Guide on page 138 for advice on camera specifications and any accessories you may need.

SET THE SCENE: ESTABLISHING SHOTS

YOU'LL NEED...

- A camera

- A tripod is helpful

- Actors, if you want them

The first shot movie makers will often choose for their movies is an **ESTABLISHING SHOT**. This is to show us where the action in the movie takes place.

Establishing Shots are usually filmed as **WIDE SHOTS**, which means that the camera can see a wide range of the set or location, as well as the full body of any main characters. Establishing Shots could also include signs.

+ Decide on where your movie takes place. You can show us Establishing Shots from real life or you can create your own set to tell us we're in a fictional place.

+ Depending on your ideas, you may need to build a set. Be creative with your ideas!

+ Think about your characters. You might want to include characters in your Establishing Shot. You don't have to, but sometimes it helps tell the story.

PRO TIPS

+ Keep the camera steady. Use a tripod or try resting your camera on a flat, steady surface.
+ Try not to film outside your set, or we lose the illusion.
+ If you've mastered a static (still) shot, try 'panning' your camera slowly from left to right to show us even more.

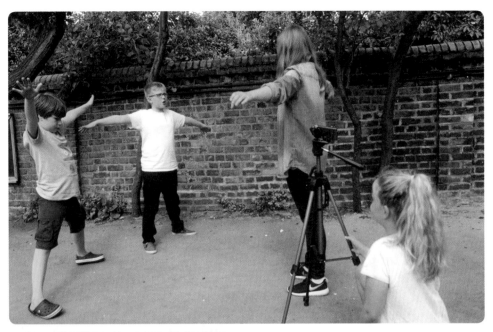

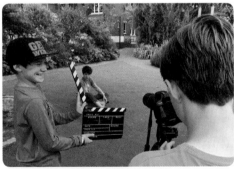

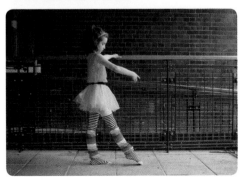

GET SHOOTING

Try these five Establishing Shots to get you started.

✦ It's your birthday party, taking place at home.
✦ At the police station, a crime is being reported.
✦ Everyone has detention at school.
✦ It seemed like a normal day at the skateboard park...
✦ Use materials like cardboard and foil to build a spaceship and shoot an Establishing Shot inside.

Now come up with your own idea and shoot your movie's Establishing Shot. **Remember:** keep it wide!

GET EMOTIONAL: USING CLOSE-UPS

YOU'LL NEED...

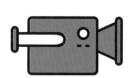 

- A camera

- An actor

One of the most useful shots you can use in your movies is the **CLOSE-UP**.

Close-ups are mostly used for showing us a character speaking or reacting in a movie. It tells us that something important is happening, and also how that character is feeling.

- ✦ Choose your character. Decide who your actor is playing and where they are.

- ✦ Direct your actor. Talk to them about what is happening and how they feel about it. Think about what they might say.

- ✦ Position your camera in front of your actor, close enough so that you can see their whole face in the screen. Zoom in until their face is the largest thing in view. Then press record.

PRO TIPS

- ✦ Get as close in as you can to your actor, before you zoom in.
- ✦ Put your camera level with your actor's eyes.
- ✦ Include a glimpse of your actor's shoulders in your shot.

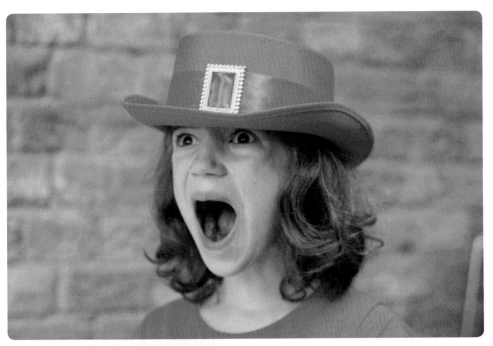

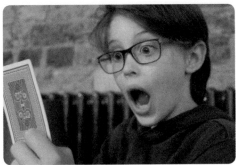

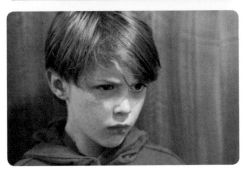

GET SHOOTING
Have a go at filming these Close-ups.

✦ Your actor sees a ghost.
✦ A doctor arrives at an accident.
✦ Your actor wins a major award.
✦ Someone finds out their best friend is leaving.
✦ Someone has just been grounded by their parents.

Have a think about your own movie and plan some Close-ups to show your character's emotions and reactions.

EXTREME CLOSE-UPS

YOU'LL NEED...

- A camera

- An actor

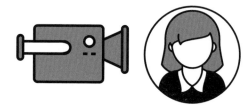

AN EXTREME CLOSE-UP SHOT is similar to a Close-up, but it is so close that it focuses on just one part of an actor's face. It usually shows us a character's eyes, or sometimes their mouth.

An Extreme Close-up is a good shot for showing intense emotion, or for creating atmosphere and style.

✦ To shoot an Extreme Close-up, you need to be very close physically to your actor. You can also use a camera's zoom function, or a 'telephoto'-lens.

✦ Try to use the zoom sparingly. It's always better to start with your camera very close to your actor and then just use the zoom as a 'top-up' if needed.

✦ Ask your actor to keep very still during an extreme closeup. Even the slightest movement of their head can mean that their eye moves out of shot.

PRO TIPS

✦ Work with your actor to exaggerate their eyes or speech until you're happy with their performance on screen.

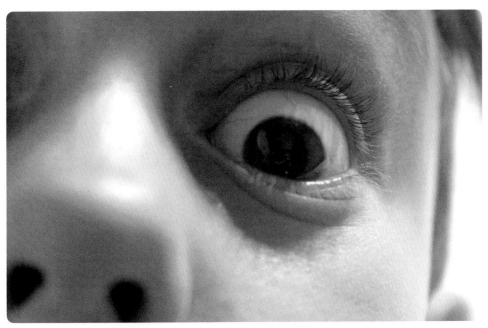

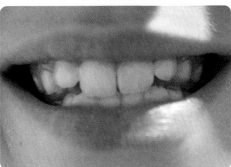

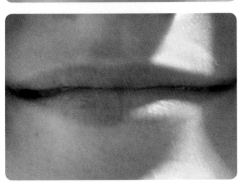

GET SHOOTING

Here are some suggested shots you can film to practise Extreme Close-ups.

- ✦ Eyes - a cowboy squints their eyes at their rival.
- ✦ Eyes - a character shows 'puppy dog eyes' and says 'Please...'
- ✦ Eyes - a superhero resolves to save the day.
- ✦ Mouth - a witch or a wizard casts a dangerous spell.

Think up some Extreme Close-ups of your own and add them to your collection.

OVER THE SHOULDER SHOTS

YOU'LL NEED...

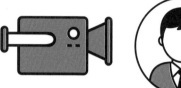 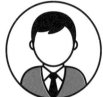

- A camera

- 2 actors

Another shot you can include in your movie is the **OVER THE SHOULDER SHOT**. This shot is useful for conversations between characters, for revealing a sense of perspective, or for showing that someone is 'being watched'.

Over the Shoulder Shots usually feature two or more actors and are named for the camera position during the shot. The shot is filmed from behind one of the characters, pointing over their shoulder. Try to include a little of their shoulder and the back of their head to line the left and the bottom of the frame.

PRO TIPS

✦ Look at the actor in front of you and find out the level of their eyes. Line your camera up with their eyeline.

✦ Practise shooting the mirror image of your shot from over the other actor's shoulder. Try to film over the opposite shoulder. If your first shot is over the right shoulder, use the second actor's left shoulder next.

GET SHOOTING

Here are some ideas for Over the Shoulder Shots.

✦ Two friends are talking about an upcoming maths test.
✦ A police officer is interviewing a suspect.
✦ A person sees a ghost.

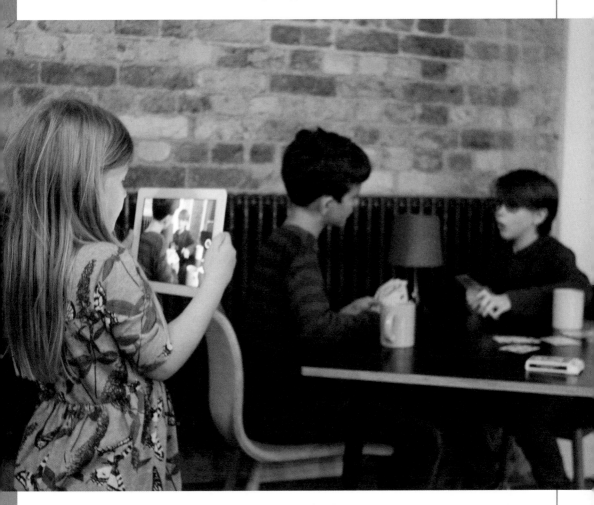

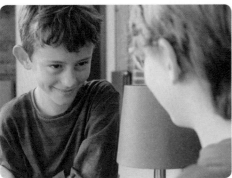

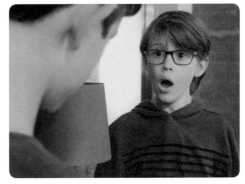

MIRROR SHOT

YOU'LL NEED...

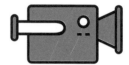

- A mirror

- A camera

This is a fun challenge that can produce some really interesting and tricky shots using reflections in a mirror.

✦ Try and position your camera so that you can see a reflection of something in a mirror. Be careful to place your camera at an angle so that the camera's reflection isn't visible in the shot.

✦ When you have the right position, film your shots in front of the mirror.

PRO TIPS

✦ You don't need to stick to mirrors: there are all sorts of reflective surfaces that can help make some interesting shots. Try filming a shot of the sky in a reflective puddle, or a reflection in somebody's sunglasses.

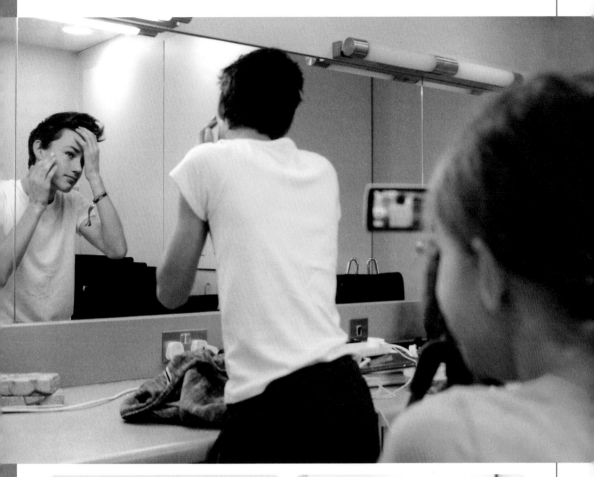

GET SHOOTING

Here are some examples of scenes to shoot through a mirrored surface.

✦ An Over the Shoulder Shot of someone talking to their reflection.

✦ A ghost arrives in the background, over your actor's shoulder.

✦ A character dressing in disguise.

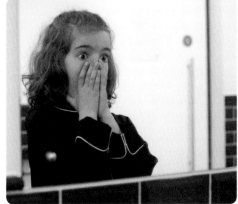

SHOOTING HIGH ANGLE SHOTS

YOU'LL NEED...

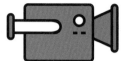

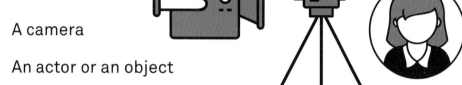

- A camera

- An actor or an object

- A tripod is helpful, but not essential

HIGH ANGLE SHOTS are filmed from a height above your actors or objects. They are often nicknamed 'Bird's Eye View' shots and can be used to give your audience different information as the perspective changes to a higher level.

A High Angle Shot can make your actors appear smaller, or a character appear more vulnerable. This can be great in helping to build suspense, to tell us about a character's status or to make us feel sorry for a character.

To film a High Angle Shot, you need to be at the right height above your actors or objects. You can stand at the top of a staircase, or on a chair, but make sure you're filming safely and ask for help.

PRO TIPS

- ✦ Use a tripod to steady your shots and for extra height.
- ✦ Experiment with different height levels to get different effects. The higher or more extreme your angle, the smaller and more vulnerable your characters become.

GET SHOOTING
Try shooting some High Angle Shots like these.

- ✦ A bird looks down at a tasty worm.
- ✦ A young character tells the camera, 'I'm sorry.'
- ✦ CCTV catches a burglar in the act.
- ✦ A child is lost, alone and scared.

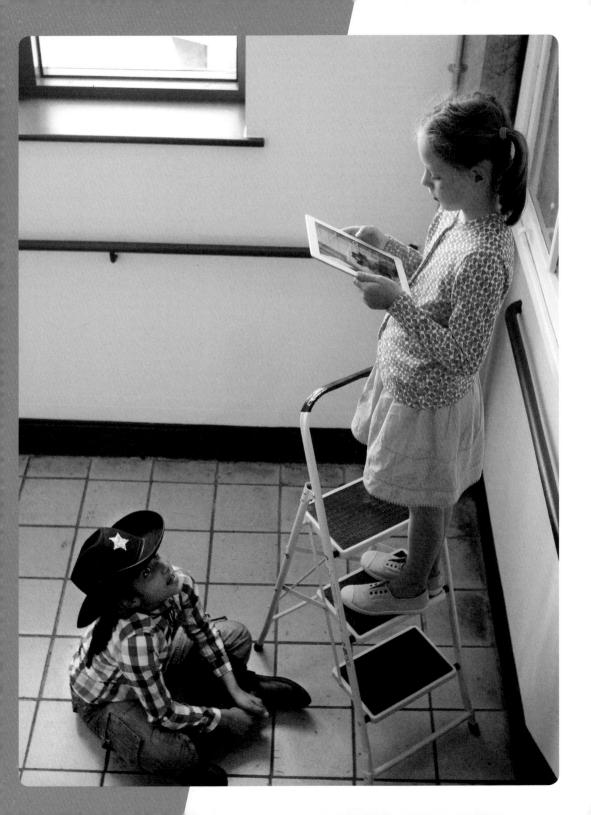

SHOOTING LOW ANGLE SHOTS

YOU'LL NEED...

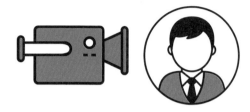

- A camera

- An actor or an object

A LOW ANGLE SHOT is the opposite of a High Angle Shot. It is filmed from below and is often called a 'Worm's Eye View' shot.

A Low Angle Shot can be used to give a character or an object higher status, as they appear larger and more dominant in the frame when filmed from below.

To shoot a Low Angle Shot, position your camera below your actor or object, usually below the actor's eyeline or the base of the object.

PRO TIPS

✦ Consider going 'hand held' instead of using a tripod. This way you can position your camera closer to the ground. If you're very low down, you might also want to hold the camera with your hand pointing downwards rather than upwards to make it a little more comfortable.

✦ Your camera may have a viewing screen that will tilt towards you. This may be more comfortable for viewing a shot while filming from low down.

✦ Experiment with different height levels to get different effects. The lower or more extreme your angle, the more powerful your characters become.

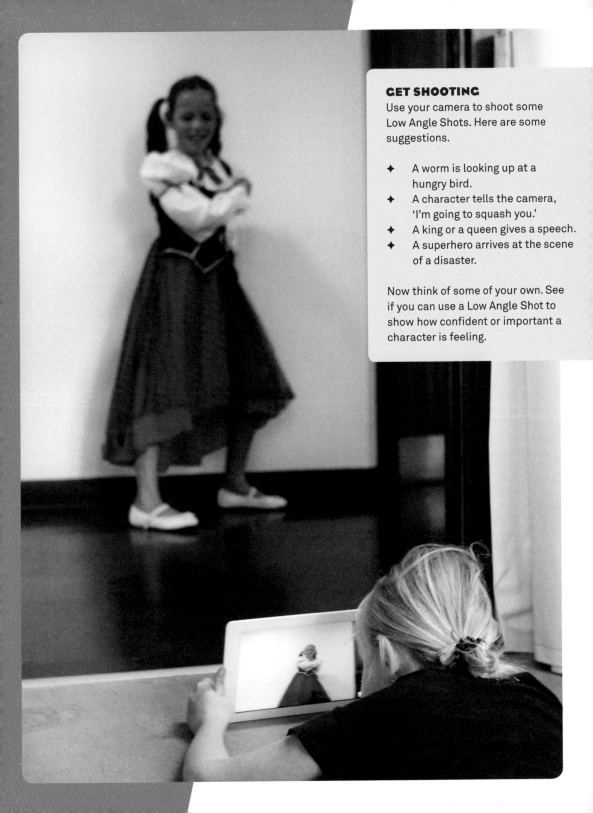

GET MOVING: TRACKING SHOTS

YOU'LL NEED...

- A camera

- An actor

- Space to move around in

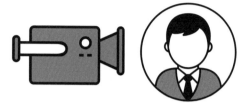

In a **TRACKING SHOT**, the camera moves to follow a character, or 'tracks' around a space. Often a Tracking Shot follows a character on a journey, with the actor and the camera moving together so the character stays in the frame.

Tracking Shots give motion and pace, so they are perfect for action movies. Tracking shots can be filmed 'hand held', or on a tripod attached to a dolly (a kind of trolley on wheels). A good alternative dolly is a chair with wheels - ask someone to help move the chair while you film.

PRO TIPS

- ✦ Tracking shots can be tricky to get right, because they rely on so much movement. It's usually a good idea to rehearse your shot a few times before filming.
- ✦ Avoid using the zoom while filming a Tracking Shot as this can be confusing to your audience.
- ✦ Think about your backgrounds, and be careful not to get any crew members in the shot as you move around the space.

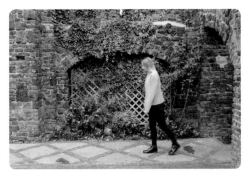

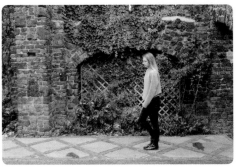

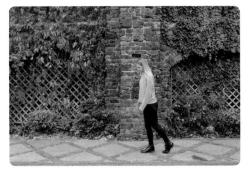

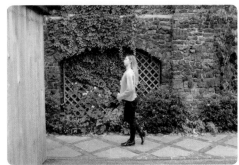

GET SHOOTING

Here are some suggested Tracking Shots. Use your camera to try filming them.

✦ Shoot a person running along the pavement.
✦ Track an explorer in your garden.
✦ Track 360º around a character standing still.
✦ Shoot your character face-on to the camera, tracking backwards.

Now think of some Tracking Shots of your own and give them a try!

THE BIG REVEAL: USING TILT SHOTS

YOU'LL NEED...

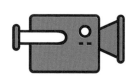 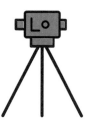 

- A camera

- An actor

- A tripod is helpful, but not essential

A TILT SHOT moves vertically, up and down. It can start high and tilt lower, or it can start low and tilt higher. It creates the same effect as a person lifting or lowering their head.

This type of shot is good for 'reveals' about characters: for example, we might see a pair of feet and slowly tilt up a character's body to eventually reveal their face. This technique can help create lots of suspense. It's also a great shot for emphasising how tall something is, or following something that moves up and down – like a yo-yo.

✦ When shooting a Tilt Shot you'll need to practise a very steady, controlled movement.

✦ Make sure the camera doesn't zoom in or out, or moves from side to side.

✦ You might want to pause at the beginning and end of the movement rather than start tilting straight away, so the audience will have time to see what's going on!

✦ If you're using a tripod you'll need to make sure the tilting handle is loose (and the other ones are tight).

PRO TIPS

+ Use a tripod to get a smooth tilt action and a steady shot.
+ Rehearse the shot with your actor to get their best performance.
+ Before shooting, do a rehearsal and check the framing of the shot at the end of the sequence as well as the beginning. You want it to look beautiful all the way through.

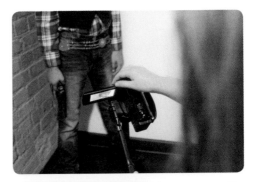

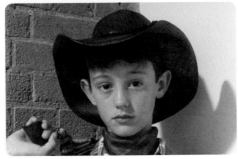

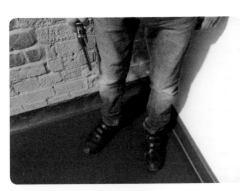

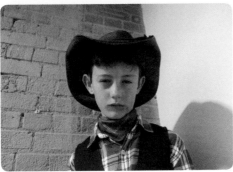

GET SHOOTING
Try filming some of these Tilt Shots.

+ A cowboy arrives at the saloon. Begin by filming their feet and tilting up to reveal whose they are.
+ Your character is late for school. Begin by filming their face, then tilt down to reveal that they are wearing mis-matching shoes.
+ A basketball player jumps to throw for the hoop. Begin with their feet on the floor and tilt up as they jump.
+ Film a tall building from the ground and then tilt up to reveal how tall it is.

SHOOT A TROMBONE SHOT

YOU'LL NEED...

- A camcorder

- An actor (or a prop will do)

- Space to move around in with a distinctive background (plain walls will not work for this).

This is a great technique to add some pizazz to a scene where a character experiences something shocking, intriguing, upsetting or just bizarre.

This shot is a tricky one to master and a good challenge for people who feel very comfortable with a camcorder. In a **TROMBONE SHOT** the person in the shot stays the same size but the background grows or shrinks in an unusual way. In our example, take a look at the two images of the boy. Notice how in the second image we can see a wider background including the bricks on either side of the trellis, but the boy hasn't changed size in the shot.

This can be very hard to get right, so film every rehearsal just in case it works first time!

✦ Ask your actor to stay still and to act shocked. Use your camera to frame them in a **MID SHOT** (from waist height). Make sure your camera is fully zoomed out.

✦ Slowly, walk backwards away from your actor, while steadily zooming in on them. You are aiming for your walking backwards to be the same speed as the camera zooming in. It is really important to get the speeds absolutely right, as the effect only works when the two speeds match.

✦ Once you have mastered this, try the other way around: start with the camera zoomed in, and then walk towards your actor and zoom out.

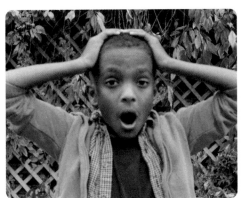

GET SHOOTING
Once you've mastered the technique, why not put it into practice with a few of these scenes?

✦ A character witnesses an alien spacecraft landing.
✦ A character is hypnotised.
✦ A character hears something moving under the bed...

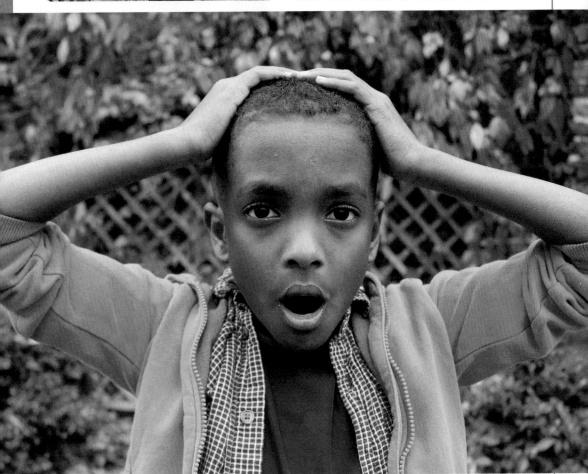

MOVIE
SKILLS

Once you've mastered a great range of shots, it's time to find out how to put them together and make a movie.

The best movies have characters that the audience love (or hate) and gripping stories that keep them hooked to the very last scene. In this section you will find lots of ideas for coming up with characters your audience will believe in, and learn how to write a script just like professional movie makers.

You'll also discover storyboards: what they are, how they work and how to use all your different types of shots to create a good one. Then you can bring all these skills together on your own amazing movie projects.

CREATE CRACKING CHARACTERS

YOU'LL NEED...

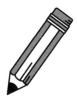

- A pen and paper
- Props for inspiration!
- Newspapers or magazines

The best movies are always about interesting characters. Whether we love them or hate them, we're always interested in what they are going to do next. There are lots of different ways in which you can start creating interesting characters. Have a look at the suggestions below to get you going.

CREATE YOUR CHARACTERS

✦ Go on an adventure. Characters are usually on some sort of journey. Sometimes it's a physical journey, for instance an astronaut travelling in space. Choose a location and try to imagine a character who lives there, who travels there, or who finds themselves there accidentally. Think about who they are, and try to write a description of your character and their adventure. What do they discover on the way?

✦ Collect some inspiration props from around the house. Try to find things from outside your bedroom, and make sure you have permission to use anything you find. Gather your props together and think about why they might be important to a person, or an animal, or why the character might use these items. See what happens if you combine different props. Write a description of your character and why these items are important to them. Try to build a story around your character and that item.

✦ Find some magazines (or newspapers) and have a look for photographs of people inside them. Try to avoid using famous people, if you can. Cut the people out and

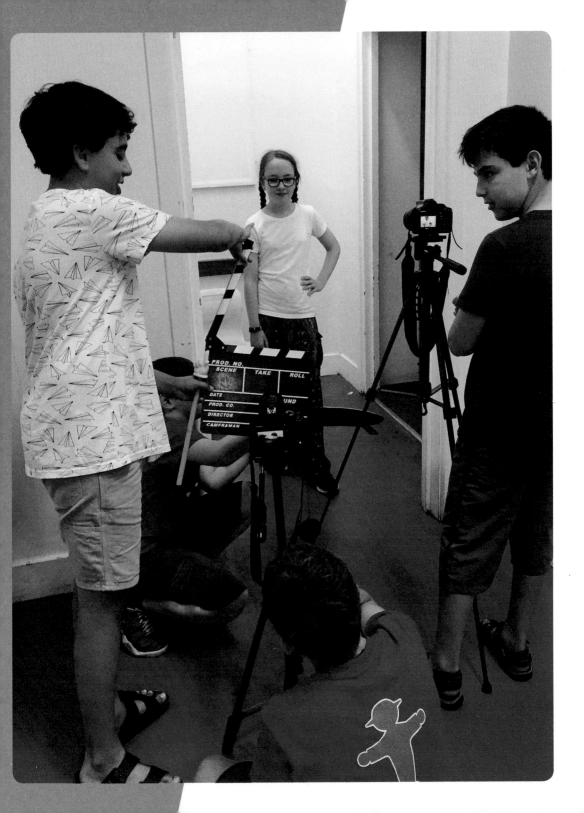

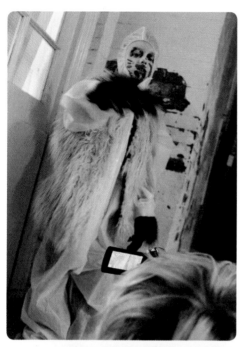

PRO TIPS

✦ As a warm-up activity, see if you can interview your characters on camera so you get to know them a little bit better. Ask them personal questions that will help you to understand more about them.

✦ Give your characters physical and emotional traits, or words or phrases that they use a lot when speaking. This will help to make them more 'three-dimensional' and believable to your audience.

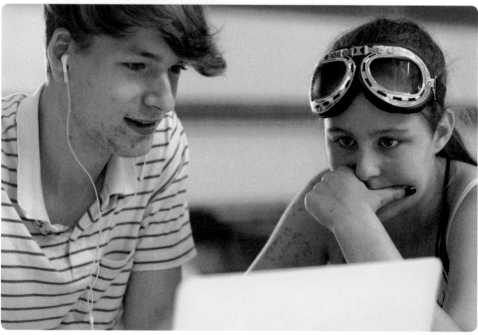

stick them onto a piece of plain paper. Try to imagine them in real life and invent three facts about each person. Next, have a think about how the cutout characters might know one another.

GIVE THEM A STORY

Now you have the basis of some movie characters, it's time to make them even more interesting...

✦ Give them a goal. Think about what they want to achieve and what motivates them to do things.

✦ Give them a flaw, or a surprising trait that you don't expect them to have. Perhaps your hero is very brave, but terrified of spiders. Maybe your villain is ruthless towards people, but compassionate towards animals. Try to make your character's flaw connected to their goal if you can.

✦ Start thinking about your character's story. Where do they start off in their journey, and where will they end? Think about an 'arc' for your character, a way for them to transform through your story. Decide how they can overcome their flaw, or whether they can they find a way to work around it. Consider

their goal and if it changes in your story, or if there is anything you would like them to learn. Map out how your character might change as a result of the things that happen to them.

✦ Make things difficult for your character. Think about what could happen in your story that would put your character under pressure. See if you can invent some circumstances for them that will make it harder for them to achieve their goal. Be as mean as you possibly can to your character – it will make your audience like them even more!

✦ Give them a nemesis (an opponent or bad guy). Invent a second character using any of the methods above, or based around your main character's goal or flaw. Superhero movies offer lots of great examples of nemesis characters.

✦ Now you have developed your characters to be the most interesting versions of themselves, you can start creating movies around them.

SIZZLING SCRIPTS

YOU'LL NEED...

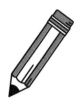

- A pencil and paper

- A word-processing programme

This project will help you write a professional-looking movie script in preparation for shooting your movie masterpiece.

Scripts are used by movie crews, directors and actors to get ready for filming. They tell the story, help directors to imagine how the movie will look and help actors to learn their lines.

KNOW YOUR STORY

✦ First, you should have a story. Start your script by noting down your story, separating it into a beginning, a middle and an end. Keep it simple and precise and try using bullet points to make it clear.

✦ Write down a list of your characters and how they relate to one another.

✦ In the beginning, you should establish who your characters are, where your movie takes place, and what is 'normal life' for everyone concerned.

✦ In the middle, something usually changes that sets your main character (or a group) off on a journey or a mission.

✦ In the end, something happens that means your main character's journey comes to an end. Consider if you would like a happy ending, or a tragic one.

SCENE BREAKDOWNS

✦ Next, break your story down into 'scenes'. A scene takes place in one location and at one time; for instance, 'Scene 1 happens in a classroom at 3.30pm'. Each scene

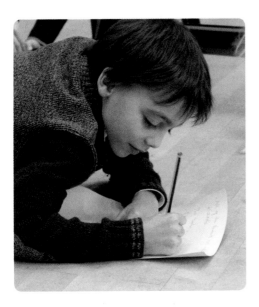

PRO TIPS

✦ Think carefully about your dialogue and try to keep it naturalistic. Listen to how people around you talk in real life and see if you can write following that style. Avoid lengthy monologues; try to keep dialogue punchy and to the point.

✦ Look at the Create your Characters project on page 32. Try to give each of your characters individual traits and ways of speaking. Build this into your dialogue and the way your characters behave.

✦ Try working with different time frames to give your script an interesting 'non-linear' structure. For instance, try using flashbacks, or starting your movie at the end.

should have its own beginning, middle and end, and should contribute towards the overall story.

✦ You can have as many scenes as you like, but usually the middle has more scenes than the beginning or the end.

✦ Decide where each scene takes place and which characters are involved. Make a note of what happens and what each character does in the scene.

START YOUR SCRIPT

Now, it's time to start writing your script. Choose a scene and describe how it begins.

Start by telling us:
✦ the Scene Number, e.g. '1'
✦ if it takes place inside ('INT' for Interior) or outside ('EXT' for Exterior)
✦ where it takes place, e.g. School playground
✦ when it takes place, e.g. Lunch time.

YOUR SCENE HEADING SHOULD LOOK SOMETHING LIKE THIS:

'1. EXT. SCHOOL PLAYGROUND. LUNCH TIME.'

Next, give us a brief description of what is happening. For example:

'The STUDENTS are standing in a circle, holding hands.'

Now, write your dialogue, giving each line to specific characters. Dialogue is the speech that your characters say. For example:

'SARA
That's not fair!'

Add in any directions or visual elements you would like to see within your movie. For example:

'SARA storms off towards the staff room.'

✦ Keep going, adding in the dialogue and the directions until you reach the end of your scene. Remember, try to give each scene its own beginning, middle and end, and make sure that everything you write contributes towards your story.

✦ When you have finished one scene, move onto the next one until you have a complete movie.

✦ As a guideline, one page of script roughly equals one minute of movie time, or a little more if your page is filled with action rather than dialogue. If you would like your movie to be 20 minutes long, aim for approximately 20 pages of script.

FORMATTING YOUR SCRIPT
Professional movie scripts follow a very particular layout. Take a look at the example above to format your script according to the rules.

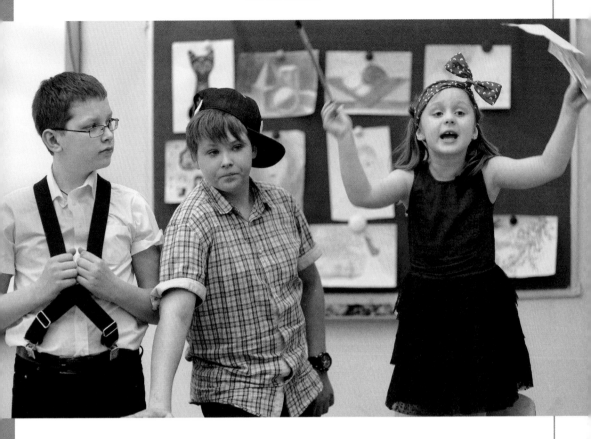

✦ Character names should appear in capital letters and in bold.

✦ Dialogue should appear in the centre of the page, with the name of the character speaking above it.

✦ Directions or visual elements should be aligned to the left side of the page.

✦ Space your writing out, so there is a lot of room for people to make notes on the page (this is useful for directors and actors, when they study your script).

✦ If you are working on a word processor, the best font to use is Courier or Courier New. This is the font used for most professional movie scripts.

You should now be ready to write a complete script... Good luck!

MAKING A STORYBOARD

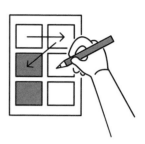

YOU'LL NEED...

- A storyboard template

- A pencil or pen

Once you have written a movie scene, the next step is to break it down into individual shots using a **STORYBOARD**. A storyboard is a series of pictures that help movie makers explain to the rest of their film crew how they want a scene to be shot. It helps you to prepare and organise your movie.

It's always a good idea to choose your shots before you start filming a movie. Think carefully about what you want to show your audience, which shots are best to do this, and how to sequence them creatively to make up your movie.

PRO TIPS

✦ Draw in pencil first (so it's easy to change) and then outline in pen once you're happy with your choices.

✦ Think about colour themes. Colour choices can give us a certain feel or tell us about a character. Experiment with colouring in your storyboard or making 'swatch notes' for each shot

✦ Include helpful details in your notes. Pro movie makers often work with a large crew, and a well-thought-out storyboard will help you to communicate your vision to actors and any crew members you work with.

DRAW IT OUT

✦ Once you've decided on your shots, draw them out on the storyboard so you can see how they might look on screen.

✦ Pay attention to the size of each shot. For instance, if you want to include a Close-up of an actor's face, then draw their face large in the frame.

✦ If you want to include an Over the Shoulder Shot, make sure you include the actor's shoulder in your sketch.

✦ You can use the box underneath, as well as the space around the frame, to make notes. These can be descriptions of your shots, notes of any actions for the actors to perform, or dialogue (speech) they might say.

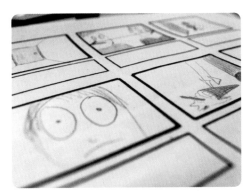

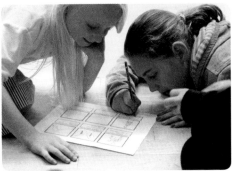

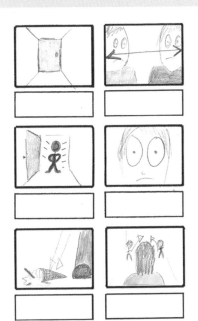

A SCENE OF SUSPENSE

✦ Establishing Shot of a door at the end of a corridor.

✦ Shot of two children – a knock at the door.

✦ The door opens – dramatic sound effect...

✦ Extreme Close-up of scared child's face.

✦ Tilt Shot as ice cream falls from the child's hand

✦ Over the Shoulder Shot of person entering the room.

SPECIAL
FX
SHOTS

In this section there are lots of tricks and techniques that will help you recreate some impressive stunts and special effects.

You will be surprised how easy it is to see like an animal, vanish into thin air, survive an earthquake, climb a mountain or sail a stormy sea. You can create some fantastic feats with little more than just your camera and a steady hand.

These projects will work well as mini movies, or you can work them into part of a longer movie. With a little practice you could make the next action-packed blockbuster classic.

MAKING GIANTS

YOU'LL NEED...

- A camera

- An actor

- Another actor (or a toy)

- A good amount of space

~~~~~~

This activity plays with perspective to create some really simple but impressive special effects. If you don't have two actors you can use a soft toy or a plastic model in place of the first (close-up) actor.

✦ Ask your first actor to stand close to your camera. This person will be your 'giant'.

✦ Next, ask your second actor to stand really far away, but somewhere that you can still see them through the camera. The idea is to make the second person look small enough to fit into your giant's hand.

✦ Ask your giant to hold their hand up and in the correct position to make the trick look convincing. It may take some directing to get your actors to pose in exactly the right place.

PRO TIPS

✦ Once you've mastered this technique you can experiment with lots of variations. Try making a toy spaceship look big enough for a person to fit aboard.

✦ Make a movie using this technique. Try telling a story about tiny people in a land of giant objects.

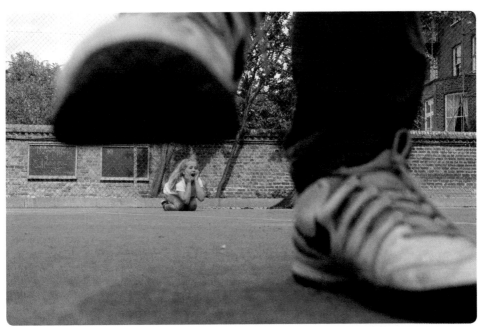

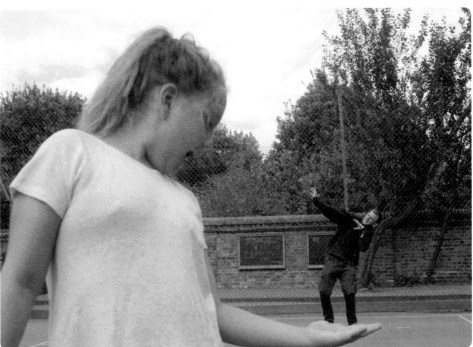

VANISHING SHOTS

YOU'LL NEED...

- A camera

- A tripod

- An actor

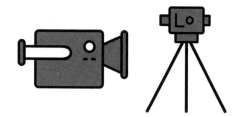

This special effect technique makes things appear and disappear in front of your audience's eyes, like a magic vanishing trick.

It's a good idea to use a tripod or something steady to rest your camera on, as the camera needs to stay really still for this effect to work.

In this example we'll use an actor to play a witch who is going to cast a spell and disappear. Instead of an actor, you could use a toy or a plasticine model.

✦ Ask your witch to stand in front of your chosen background. It's a good idea to use a **WIDE SHOT** for this effect.

✦ Film your actor casting a spell, clicking their fingers or waving a magic wand.

✦ Press the Stop button, being really careful not to move the camera or change the angle in any way.

✦ Ask your actor to leave the shot (again making sure you don't move the camera).

✦ Start recording again, filming just the background location without your actor in it.

When you play your footage back you should see your actor vanishing in an instant.

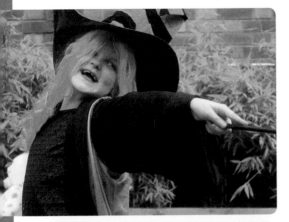

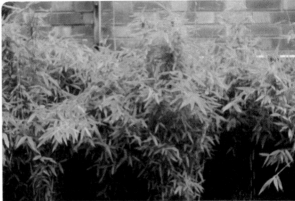

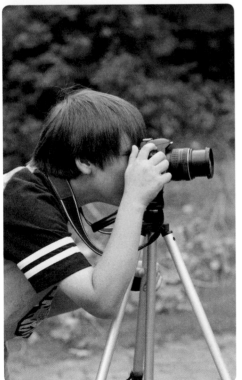

PRO TIPS

✦ Once you have mastered this trick you could try it in reverse, by filming your actor re-appearing somewhere else.

✦ Try some variations: make your actor change costume in an instant, or make a prop magically appear in their hands. Remember to ask your actor to be very still!

✦ This shot won't work so well if there are things moving around behind the actor.

CLIFFHANGERS!

YOU'LL NEED...

- A camera
- An actor
- Access to outside space
- Rope or string

This special effect is a favourite for action blockbuster directors. Using clever film angles, you'll make it look as though your actor is climbing up an extremely steep cliff.

✦ Choose a background for the shot. The background is crucial for this trick to work. Try to pick somewhere where the ground looks like a cliff or wall – a gravelly garden path, or paving stones can work really well. Think creatively and explore the garden or park to see if you can find a space that looks as though it might be found next to a cliff. A hedge can look good, or a lovely open view of the sky is ideal.

✦ Now, put your camera as close as you can to the floor. While looking through your camera, tilt it until the ground appears to slope upwards. The camera will be a bit 'wonky' – filmmakers call this a **CANTED ANGLE**. Watch out for anything in the background that might give away the effect.

✦ Now position your actor and ask them to crawl or scramble along the ground as if they are climbing up the cliff face. Make sure to tell them which way is 'up', so they climb in the right direction.

✦ Film the ground, your actor and a bit of the background (or sky). This will help the audience see all of the action properly.

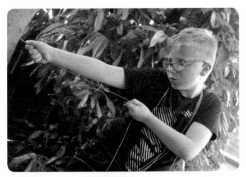

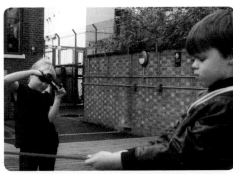

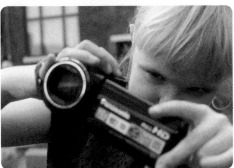

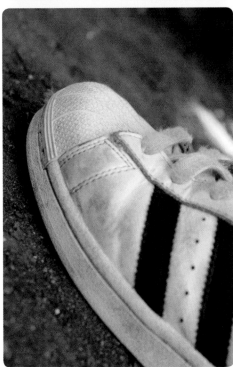

PRO TIPS

+ You might want to ask your actor to use a rope or other props to make their climb look more realistic. Ask an extra crew member for help with holding the rope so it's tight and at the right angle.

+ Once they've climbed up, why not ask your actor to roll back down the cliff for a funny comedy ending!

SAILING AWAY

YOU'LL NEED...

- A cardboard box (or something that can represent the side of a boat)

- An actor

- A camera

- A pirate or sailor's costume

This camera trick takes your audience on a voyage across the sea. The technique uses **CANTED ANGLES**, like in the Cliffhangers project (see page 48). This time, the camera gently swings from one angle to the other, giving the impression of swaying. This will create a rocking motion that will suggest the boat is at sea!

✦ Find something to represent the side of a boat: a decorated cardboard box or light plank of wood works perfectly.

✦ Ask your actor to sit behind the prop so that they look as if they are in the boat. Dress them in a sailor costume, or try a pirate's eye patch and telescope.

✦ Film your shot. Swing the camera from left to right and back again several times. Lift your left hand higher and then your right. Ask your actor to move along with the motion, moving in the same direction as the rough sea waves throw about their character!

✦ Be careful not to film the floor, and angle the shot so you have the sky in the background. Try to avoid any nearby buildings so as not to spoil the illusion that we're out in the open sea.

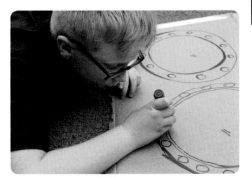

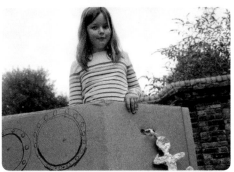

PRO TIPS

+ Be careful to avoid silhouettes. When filming against the sky your actors might start to look silloheutted against the light. If this happens, turn everything around to face away from the light, or find some extra light (from a torch, or reflector board) to make sure we can see your actor's face.

+ Try to move the camera slowly, or your audience might start to feel seasick.

+ Use this technique to make a movie about a pirate or a sailor, set aboard their ship.

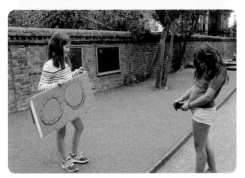

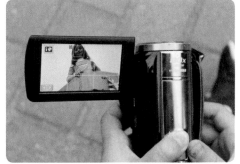

DANGER! EARTHQUAKE!

YOU'LL NEED...

- A camera

- A tripod

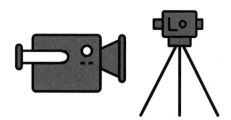

This special effect creates a convincing earthquake, perfect for making disaster movies.

✦ Choose a set or a location. It's a good idea to shoot in a place without too many props or any background furniture, as in a real earthquake these would fall over and you don't want to give the illusion away.

✦ Press the Record or Start button to begin filming. Using two hands, wobble the legs of your tripod, so that the camera shakes rapidly on the spot.

✦ Experiment with different size shakes, and which direction to move the camera. Placing your camera on a tripod will help you get a nice controlled shake as you

don't want the camera to swing wildly. Instead, aim for very little movements that happen quickly.

PRO TIPS

✦ Add some other shots to make a short disaster sequence. Try to show characters arriving at the scene in a Wide Shot and then reacting to the earthquake in Close-up. Film your shots in sequence and then try editing them together with sound effects to make a mini disaster movie.

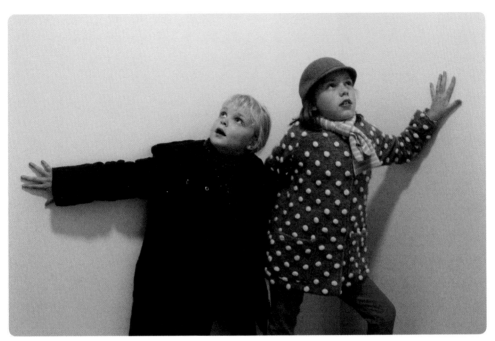

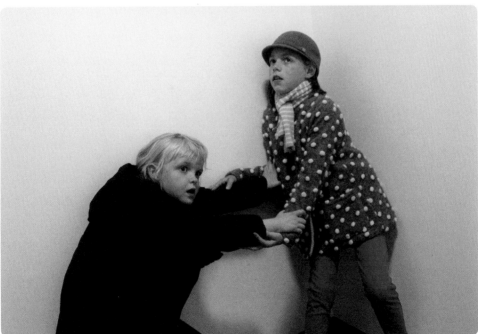

EDITING YOUR MOVIES

In this section, you'll find lots of ideas and projects to build up your skills in movie editing. Editing is an exciting part of movie making. It's where you start to piece your movie together and combine all the different shots you've filmed to tell your story. In the process, you'll see your movie take shape, and you'll add everything you need to turn a collection of shots into a finished movie.

Editors take footage (clips you have filmed) and decide in which order the audience should watch the clips, and how to arrange them to make sure everyone enjoys the finished movie and also understands what is going on. Editing helps to create mood, atmosphere, style, emotional impact and suspense. By exploring the projects in this section, you'll learn how to show flashbacks, create slow-motion effects and add in green-screen visual tricks.

You'll need some basic editing software, such as a desktop or laptop programme, or an app. See the Equipment Guide on page 139 for suggestions on which ones to look out for.

TIME-HOPPING TRANSITIONS

YOU'LL NEED...

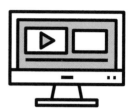

- Editing software or app

- Footage to experiment with

This project experiments with editing **TRANSITIONS**.

Transitions are the ways that shots change from one to another in a film. The most common transition is the most basic one, which is a **STRAIGHT CUT**. In a straight cut the screen jumps from one shot to another immediately.

When you're editing a film, you might want to make a change to the time frame. For example, you might want to show that some time has passed between events, or that the next scene happened a long time ago. Perhaps a character is having a vision of the future. We can use transitions to tell the audience that we're moving through time.

FADES AND DISSOLVES

If a long time has passed between two scenes you can use a **FADE**. A fade takes the first shot and then gradually makes the image darker until it fades out and is just a black screen. A fade can also fade in, which works the opposite way. The screen starts black and then gradually brings in the shot. Putting a fade in between two shots is a great way to tell the audience that two scenes happen on different days, weeks or even years. A **DISSOLVE** transition is similar, but instead of fading to a black screen, a dissolve blends one shot gradually into another. This also has the effect of time passing by.

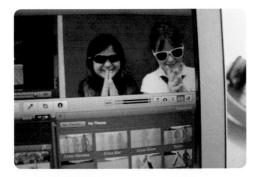

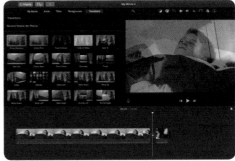

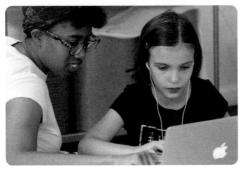

PRO TIPS

✦ Try not to use too many special transitions in one film, as this can distract attention away from the story. It's better to use one effect consistently.

RIPPLES Sometimes you might want to move time in an unusual way. For instance, you might want to show a dream of the future, or to take the audience back in time. A wobbly transition like a ripple can show that time is moving in an unusual way. With a ripple transition the two shots wave in and out to transform in a dream-like motion.

There are lots of transitions to choose from, so explore and see what you can do to take your characters on a journey through time.

TRANSISTION TRYOUTS

✦ Experiment with different transitions to give the impression of time travelling backwards and forwards. In your editing programme, add the transitions between different shots until you get the effect you're looking for.

✦ Once you have inserted your transition, experiment with speed and timings. If a transition takes longer it can make the movement seem more gradual, while a quick transition will make the story feel like it's moving much faster.

ACTION REPLAY

YOU'LL NEED...

- Footage of something physical like a sports match

- Basic editing software

~~~~~~~~~~~~~~~~~~~~~~~~~~~~

In an action replay, the audience watch a clip once and then the editors repeat the action in slow motion to emphasise it.

✦ Once you have your footage uploaded, watch it back and pick out some key moments that you'd like to emphasise. You're looking for some fancy footwork, an impressive stunt or the winning goal – something that would be fun to watch again.

✦ Add your clip into the movie twice. Select the second version of the clip and then change its speed settings to slow it down. Be sure to alter only the key moments of action, as watching the whole scene in slow motion will take a long time and spoil the fun for your audience!

✦ If you have shot the scene from more than one camera, using Close-ups for slow-motion sections can really emphasise the details.

✦ You can also add an **'ACTION REPLAY'** title to make it look like something you'd see on the television!

✦ Why not experiment with speeding other sections up, so that the audience watch moments fast and then slow. These contrasts can really enhance your footage!

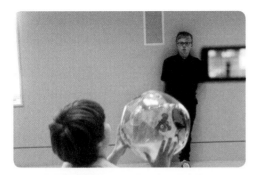
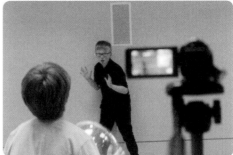
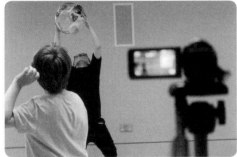
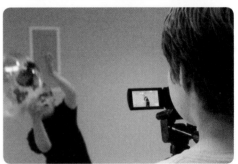
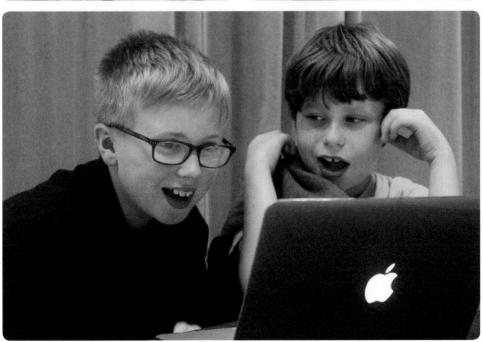

COVER THE CRACKS WITH A CUTAWAY

YOU'LL NEED...

- A camera
- A room with a clock in it
- A tripod
- An actor (this can be you!)
- Basic editing software

CUTAWAY is a term used for a shot that interrupts another shot. There are lots of reasons to use a Cutaway, but a good reason is to hide a gap in the action of a film. When you are editing, you might decide to get rid of a certain part of the footage (for example, an actor coughing in the middle of one of their lines). However, if you take something from the middle of a clip then the audience will notice a sudden jump in the footage. The actor might have been holding a cup before she coughed, and after the cough she ended up putting the cup down. If we delete the cough, the audience will suddenly see the cup 'jumping' from her hand to the table. A Cutaway can be used a bit like a plaster, smoothing over the jump so the audience doesn't notice that anything is missing.

In this project you will shoot two simple shots and then edit them together.

SHOOTING

- ✦ A **WIDE SHOT** of your actor sitting down on a chair, looking around, tapping their fingers and looking impatient. After two minutes of waiting, they get up and leave the scene.

- ✦ A **CLOSE-UP** of the clock. Make sure we can really clearly see the hands of the clock moving around.

EDITING

+ Upload your footage into your editing package.

+ Select your Wide Shot and place this on to your project timeline.

+ Watch it back and note which bits are the boring bits to watch.

+ Select a section of the middle of the shot that includes your boring bits. Make sure you keep the beginning where the actor takes a seat, and the ending where they leave.

+ Delete the selection.

+ Now watch back your footage and notice the jump in the footage from where you've deleted something. This is called a 'jump cut' and is really noticeable to audiences.

+ Next, select some of your footage of the clock. Place this in between the two parts of your clip on the timeline.

+ Watch it back. The video should cut from the shot of your actor to the shot of the clock and then back again. You have now created a Cutaway! You will see it is less noticeable that you have deleted some footage from the scene.

+ It is really good filmmaking practice to always shoot a Cutaway: they are really handy for covering mistakes and missing bits of footage.
+ Have a think about films you've made previously. Make a list of any of these that need a Cutaway to cover up some cracks.
+ Cutaways aren't always used like this. They can be used to add tension and drama to a scene. For example, in a spy film a Cutaway to a ticking bomb will remind the audience of our hero's time running out.

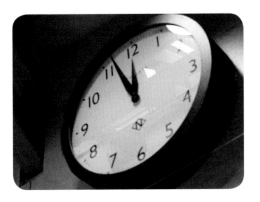

TRAVEL THE WORLD

YOU'LL NEED...

- A camera

- A green screen or a blue screen (or a plain green or blue sheet)

- Any props

- Background footage or images (.jpg or similar) from different locations around the world

- Actors

- Editing software or an editing app

Use a green screen (or a blue screen) to take you on adventures around the world. In this project, you'll look at how to shoot and edit using Chroma Key to create limitless possibilities!

With a green or blue screen, you can edit out the 'real' backgrounds and replace them with other images or fantastical backgrounds, such as an alien landscape, the inside of a volcano or the walls of a fairy castle. There are no limits to the places you can visit.

STORYBOARDING

✦ First, draw up a storyboard for your movie.

✦ Think about your setting and which shots you would like to include.

✦ **WIDE SHOTS** are good here for showing off your backgrounds.

✦ You might want to include another 'real' background in your film, for instance your back garden or school.

✦ Think about this when storyboarding as you may need to film your backgrounds separately.

✦ You can also think about making or drawing your background. Include this on your storyboard so that you remember to film it during your shoot.

SHOOTING YOUR FOOTAGE

✦ Once you're ready to film, you'll need to put up your green screen on a flat surface. Hang it on a wall or use supports to ensure the screen hangs smoothly.

✦ Try and pick a location with even lighting across the screen, or direct lamp lights toward your screen to balance out any uneven lighting.

✦ Position yourself or your actors in front of the screen. Make sure any costumes or clothing aren't green (or blue if using a blue screen) or they will also disappear when you are editing.

✦ When shooting, ensure that the green screen stretches right to the edges and fills the whole frame on

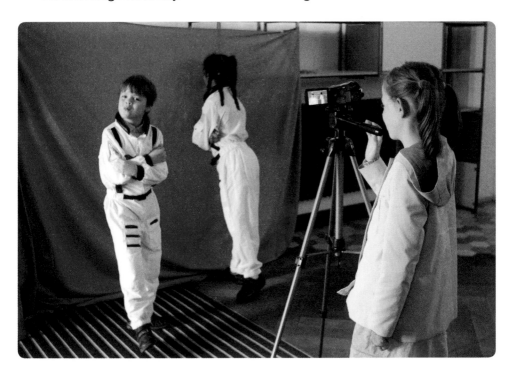

your camera. Any walls or furniture that creeps in won't disappear.

✦ Once you've shot your storyboard, along with any backgrounds, you are ready to edit!

✦ Transfer your footage to your editing programme or app.*

ADD YOUR FOOTAGE

✦ Sequence your footage in your editing programme or app.

✦ Most Chroma Key functions work by layering the footage on top of other footage.

✦ Follow the guidance in your programme to add in your background images or video first, and then layer the green-screen footage over the top.

CHROMA KEYING

✦ Once your clips are in sequence, apply a Chroma Key effect (sometimes called Keyer or Green Screen) to the green screen clips to erase the green background.

✦ You should now see yourself (or your actors) in front of the travel

backgrounds and on holiday adventures around the world!

FINISHING TOUCHES

✦ Add in music or sound effects to complement your footage.

✦ You might want to include dinosaur roars, transport sounds, or music to accompany your travels.

✦ Add in any titles such as place names, and enjoy sharing your adventures!

* Please check your editing programme beforehand as not all applications come with Chroma Key features.

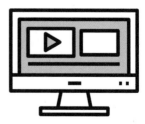

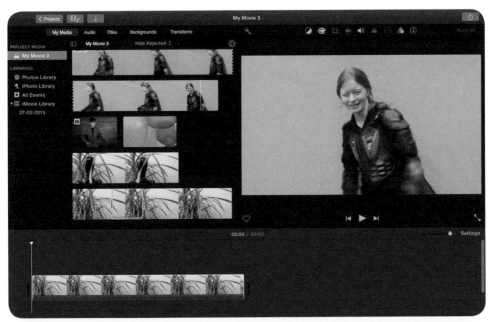

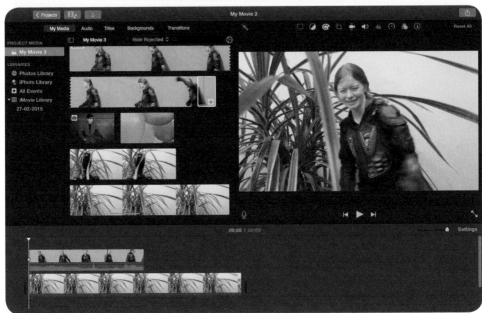

SUPER SOUNDS

Movie making isn't all about the visuals – sound is just as important. Here you'll find some useful techniques for working with sound. Good sound can give your movies a more professional finish, help to set your scene, or take your audience on an emotional journey.

When we watch a movie, the sounds that we hear can change the mood of the scene, or help us understand what is going on. Music can emphasise emotions during a scene, and sound effects can provide details about where a character is or make props and scenery feel more realistic. In this chapter you can explore different ways to make your projects sound great.

You will find tips on choosing the perfect music, how to create your own convincing sound effects and how to record your own voiceovers.

Once you've had some fun with the challenges in this chapter you could the revisit the previous movies you've worked on and apply your new skills to them.

USING MUSIC

YOU'LL NEED...

- Footage to experiment with (try using footage from your earlier movie making)

- Basic editing software

- Music files

Choosing the right music for your movie is a vital step in the production process. A great soundtrack can really enhance the overall quality and mood of your movie – and will wow your audiences.

In this project, you'll choose a piece of music and then apply it to your movie footage. With a few tweaks your movie will sound great.

✦ Watch your footage and sequence it into a scene.

✦ Think about the mood you want to share. For instance, your scene might involve lots of dramatic action, or it could be a happy ending. Also have a think about the movements: are they quick cuts, moving shots or longer static shots?

✦ Use your answers from above to describe the type of music you want to include as your soundtrack.

✦ Find your ideal music to score your scene. Most editing software comes with some music tracks to experiment with. Or, you can head to www.incompetech.com, or www. freesound.org to find more tracks to download. Have a listen to the tracks and see if they suit the mood and pace that you were looking for. If they do, then add them to your movie.

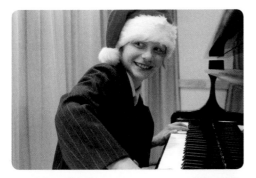

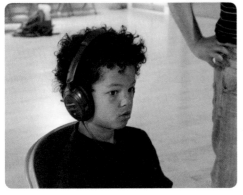

✦ Listen to the music to make sure it is at the appropriate volume. Check that you can hear crucial dialogue underneath and adjust the volume levels if you need to.

You should make sure that all of the music you include in your film is free to download and royalty free – meaning that nobody will charge you to use it! If you have any doubts, check with an adult who can help you track down where the music has come from.

PRO TIPS

✦ Consider varying the volume or the presence of music throughout your sequence. Try bringing the music in at key points in the story to emphasise emotion or to create dramatic impact. Trim the music to play it at the exact moment you want.

✦ Fade your music in and out using the volume controls. This will help to create smooth audio transitions and stop the music drawing attention to itself.

✦ Experiment with changing the tone of your movie by switching the music to something surprising. For example, if you place some lively, jolly sounding music over a scene of somebody falling over this will have a very different effect to choosing a sad violin piece. Try inserting some music that feels like the wrong choice to see the interesting effects you can create.

VOICEOVERS

YOU'LL NEED...

- Editing software or app

- Footage to experiment with (try using footage from your earlier movie projects)

- A microphone or digital audio recorder

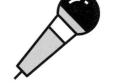

This project explores using **VOICEOVER** to communicate a character's inner thoughts. You can reveal a lot about a character using this technique.

✦ Find some earlier footage of somebody acting, but not speaking. Alternatively, you can shoot a new shot just for this project. Ask your actor to perform a task: something exciting and dramatic such as defusing a bomb, or something everyday such as washing the dishes. You could also think about using your pets for this project. Try to use a long take (a shot that goes on for a few minutes) so that you have enough time to record some interesting voiceovers.

✦ Record a voiceover so that we can hear what that person is thinking. Try to use the first person in your narrative, e.g. 'I' or 'me'.

✦ Transfer your footage and voiceover recording to your editing programme. Fine-tune by editing the voiceover to fit your movie footage, or so that key moments from the voiceover coincide with the action in your movie.

VOICEOVER IDEAS

Here are some suggested voiceover clips you could make to experiment with this technique.

- ✦ A character deciding what to wear to a party.
- ✦ A nervous character preparing to give a speech.
- ✦ A cat complaining that her humans don't feed her enough.

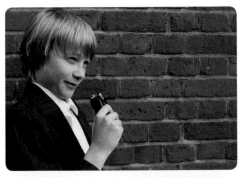

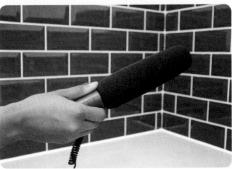

PRO TIPS

- ✦ Plan what you're going to say before you record it. You may want to make some notes or write a short script.
- ✦ When recording, do a test to check how close you should be to your microphone for the right volume. Also check for any background noise like air conditioning or electrical buzzing noises. Microphones are often more sensitive to these noises than you expect.
- ✦ Record the voiceover and then listen back to it. Listen to the volume levels, as you may need to adjust these.
- ✦ You might also want to slow down the voiceover by splitting it into separate sections.
- ✦ Explore the audio effects in your editing programme. Some editing apps have a range of different vocal effects. These can help you to change the pitch of a clip, or to put your character into an unusual environment. Consider shooting from the character's point of view for maximum impact.

FOLEY SOUND

YOU'LL NEED...

- Editing software or app

- Some footage to experiment with (try using some earlier movie footage, or shoot some scenes to match these examples)

- A microphone (your computer might have a built-in one)

- Coconut shells

- Umbrella

- Two pieces of paper

- Celery

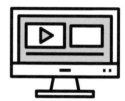

In this project, you'll create your own fun sound effects to accompany your movie footage. This technique is called **FOLEY**, which simply means making sound effects to add to a film during editing.

Sound effects can add emphasis and authenticity to a scene. They bring out details that you might not notice otherwise. Sometimes it's best to film the correct things to get a clear sound, like placing the microphone on the floor to record some footsteps. Otherwise, try making a variety of sounds near your microphone, and experiment until you create the sound you need.

The possibilities with foley are endless and foley artists are known to use really creative methods to make the perfect sound.

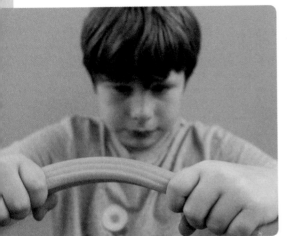
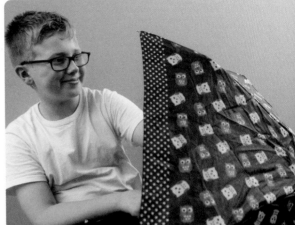

✦ Transfer your footage to your editing programme.

✦ Mute all of your footage; this will help you focus on the sounds you're going to work on. Then import your sound effects in the same way you would do for some music, or record them into your programme as you would with a voiceover (see page 71).

✦ Add in your foley effects at the right points of the action in your movie footage.

FUN WITH FOLEY

Try these example foley effects to practise your technique.

✦ Open and close an umbrella to make the sound of some bat wings flapping.

✦ Slide two pieces of paper over each other to recreate the sound of some futuristic spaceship electric doors.

✦ Two halves of a hollowed-out coconut shell make perfect clip-clopping horses.

✦ Snapping a celery stick is a great way to mimic a bone cracking in a fight scene!

MOVIE-MAKING PROJECTS

Now you have lots of movie-making skills, it's time to put them to good use in your own projects.

Here you'll find exciting ideas to start your collection of complete movie productions and your journey as an accomplished movie maker.

Each project brings a new challenge that will help to develop your creative and technical skills. There is room to bring your own imagination to each challenge so that you can celebrate your ideas and make your movies unique to you.

You'll find suggested examples to get you started and suggestions to help your with perfect planning, production techniques and editing flair. You'll also find ways to include your special-effects skills, and tips for achieving professional-looking shots in your work.

Try the projects in order, or focus on your preferred individual projects from this section. Remember to have fun and make each movie your own special creation!

FILM YOUR JOURNEY

YOU'LL NEED...

- A camera

- Basic editing software

- Permission to go for a walk (you might need to take an adult along) with your camera

~~~~~~~~~~~~~~~~~~~~~~~~~~~~~~~

This project is a great way to start thinking like a visual artist! You will capture interesting colours, patterns, sounds, shapes and objects that you pass on a walk around an area. You can these use these clips to build up a beautiful abstract representation of your journey, like a video map!

SHOOTING

✦ Don't think too much in advance about what you are going to shoot. This project works very well without lots of planning.

✦ Take your camera with you on your walk. Keep your eyes peeled for interesting sights. Walk slowly and take in everything around you.

✦ Maybe there are interesting shadows on the pavement, or birds' nests in the trees, or eye-catching signs or shopfronts.

✦ Every time something takes your eye, get your camera out and try to find an interesting way to film it. You could move the camera towards the object, or shoot it from an interesting angle. Or film it through another object like the branches of a bush.

✦ Don't film everything! Resist the urge to leave your camera on. Aim to shoot fifteen different 'moments' along your walk.

✦ Don't film other people you see - they may not like it!

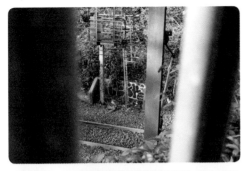

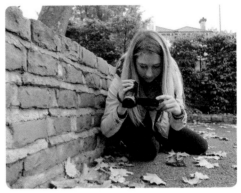

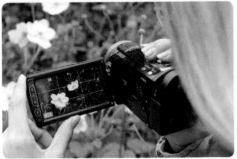

GOLDEN RULES

✦ Be really careful around roads and waterways.

✦ Always tell an adult where you are going and explain what you are up to!

EDITING

✦ Import your footage into your editing programme.

✦ Drag all your footage into your timeline. Get rid of any bits that you don't like.

✦ Now, choose some music to accompany your film. Think about your walk, what the weather was like, how quickly you moved and the kind of things you saw. Try to match the atmosphere of your journey.

✦ Place the music on to your timeline.

✦ If you want to, turn the volume down on your video clips so you can only hear the music.

✦ Watch it back, and trim any of the clips that you think are going on for too long.

✦ You might want to speed some clips up or down. You can do this to make particular moments stand out on your walk.

WHAT'S IN THE BOX?

YOU'LL NEED...

- A camera

- A box

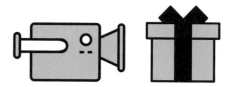

Suspense techniques work by holding information back from your audience, but slowly revealing enough that we want to know the rest. In this project, you'll shoot a short film sequence (about six shots) about 'What's In The Box.' You can show us as much of the box as you like, but don't reveal what's inside.

STORYBOARD YOUR SEQUENCE

✦ Choose your shots and draw out your storyboard in advance. Use a mixture of **WIDE SHOTS** and **CLOSE-UPS** or **CUTAWAYS** (see page 60). Think about using Point of View shots (page 96) from inside the box, or as a character approaching the box. Including a **LOW ANGLE SHOT** could give the box status.

PRE-PRODUCTION

✦ Cast any additional characters you want to include in your sequence (ask friends or family members for help) and design your box according to your story.

GET SHOOTING

✦ Following your storyboard, film your shots in order of your sequence. Remember: don't reveal what's inside the box!

POST-PRODUCTION

✦ Once you've shot your sequence, send the footage to your editing app, where you can add in music or video effects. Give your film an intriguing title and add in a title screen and credits.

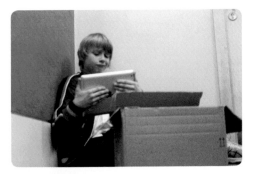

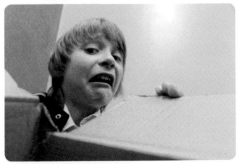

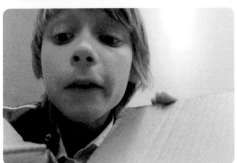

YOU MIGHT WANT TO INCLUDE

✦ Shots of the box arriving. How does it get there?
✦ Shots of the box moving.
✦ Point of View shots from inside the box.
✦ Close-up reaction shots of characters in the movie.
✦ Close-ups or Cutaways that demonstrate features of the box. Does it have a 'danger' sign? Does it have a lock?
✦ Creepy sound effects or music.

PRO TIPS

✦ Try using black-and-white or sci-fi video effects for additional creepiness.
✦ Think about timing your reveals to your music or sound effects. Can you draw particular shots out for even longer to add additional suspense?

TRAINING MONTAGE

YOU'LL NEED...

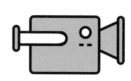
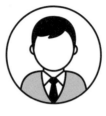
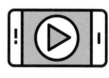

- A camera

- An actor

- Editing software or app

This project will recreate a technique that's used in lots of professional movies and television programmes. A training montage is a sequence that shows a character training for an event. This is usually physical, for instance an athlete preparing to compete in an important race or training to get on to the school basketball team.

✦ Storyboard a scene that includes a variety of shots showing your character exercising. Think about using a local adventure playground as a location and using a chin-up bar, monkey bars, ropes to swing on or ledges to hang off. Plan to capture lots of interesting **CLOSE-UPS** of hands gripping the equipment and faces with determined expressions. Also be sure to get some **WIDE SHOTS** to show the extent of the character's exercise, perhaps filming them running up and down, or doing star jumps. The more shots you can include, the better!

✦ Film your shots, making each of them a minute or longer, so you have lots of footage to edit with.

✦ Once you're happy with your shoot, open your editing programme and transfer your footage. Now sequence the clips in your movie, using all the different shots. Try to pace your shots so your audience can feel the training journey. Use sharp, quick cuts

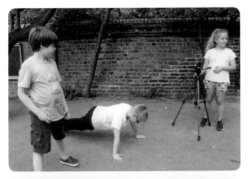

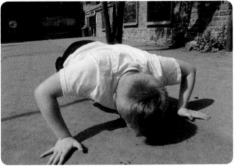

to show confidence, and longer, slower transitions to show your character's struggle.

✦ Add in transition effects, such as **DISSOLVES** and **FADES**.

✦ Choose some music and add this to your montage. Think carefully about the tempo of the music so it matches your training story.

PRO TIPS

✦ Try to order and cut your shots for variety. Swapping between longer, Wide Shots and quicker Close-ups works more effectively that lots of similar shots one after the other. Don't be afraid of using a shot more than once in a clip: you can cut back to a shot if it looks good.

✦ Try to cut your sequence to go with the beat of your music. Change your shots along with the rhythms.

✦ You might also want to show the character's progression, so maybe have the character looking exhausted in some of the shots, followed by some shots of them finding it all very easy as they grow more comfortable.

✦ You could also extend your movie: shoot a scene before and after the training, so you can establish to the audience why the character is training so hard. Perhaps they are looking at a team sign-up sheet, or talking to their coach.

PET VIDEOS

YOU'LL NEED...

- A camera

- Your pet (with permission)

- Editing software or app

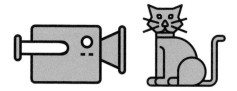

Working with animals can be challenging, but see if you can catch them doing something amazing. Find out their special talent and record it in a movie. Make sure you get permission from parents or carers first!

SHOOTING YOUR FOOTAGE

+ This is all about capturing the moment, so there isn't too much planning you can do in advance.

+ Try to set up your camera ready, so that when your pet does their trick, you can film it.

+ This might take several attempts, so be patient with your pet.

+ It's a good idea to film some **WIDE SHOTS**, so if your pet moves quickly then they'll still be in shot. Mix it up with some **CLOSE-UPS** of wagging tails, panting tongues or alert eyes, as this will make the edit more interesting.

EDITING

+ Choose your favourite takes and make a montage of your pet's performances.

+ Sequence the clips together in your editing programme and use transitions to add movement and styling.

+ Choose some fun music, or some comedy sound effects to add humour to your video.

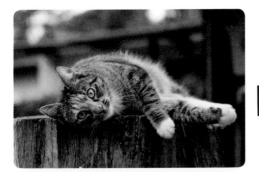

PRO TIPS

✦ Pet videos can make a great series. Revisit this project to see if you can turn your pet into a viral superstar!

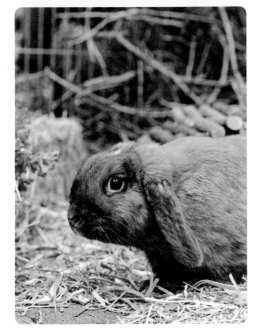

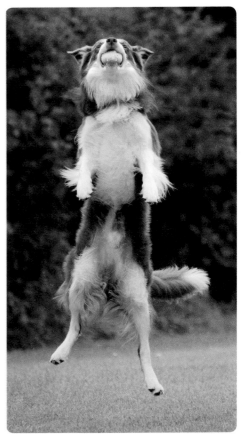

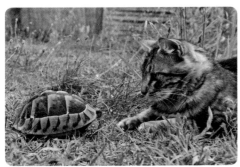

PROP CHARACTERS

YOU'LL NEED...

- A camera
- A balloon
- Editing programme or app
- Some transparent thread

Bring a prop balloon to life in a movie that doesn't have any actors or presenters.

Your mission is to give the balloon personality. Working with a lifeless balloon means working extra hard to put personality into your character, from planning your movie to editing.

Make it scary, fun or charming, but make it the star of your movie! Perhaps the balloon is sad not to be taken home from a party. Perhaps it plays tricks on people by floating up behind them, or is bored with being tied to a ribbon all day long. Have a think about a story you'd like to tell.

For inspiration, look at the movie *The Red Balloon* (1956).

STORYBOARD

- Think about which shots you would like to include in your movie and how you can show your balloon's personality.

- Consider using **HIGH** or **LOW ANGLE SHOTS**, **POINT OF VIEW SHOTS**, **TILTING**, **PANNING** or **TRACKING SHOTS**.

- Think about your colours and your set, and any movement you want to include.

- Consider how to move the balloon. Maybe you can make it drift into shot sadly (by gently blowing on it) or rush around in excitement (with an electric fan!). You can use the transparent thread to move the balloon in a way that looks as if it's moving by itself.

SHOOT YOUR FOOTAGE

✦ Once you're ready, work with your balloon to shoot through your storyboard.

✦ Rehearse your shots to achieve perfect takes ready for your edit.

✦ Once you've filmed your shots, transfer the footage to your editing programme or app.

EDITING

✦ Sequence your clips as you would like to show them, cutting between your different shots.

✦ Consider the order of your clips, along with rhythm, pacing and timing.

✦ Once you've sequenced your clips, consider adding music, or sound effects, video effects and transitions.

✦ Each choice you make should reflect the personality of your balloon to build atmosphere, mood and character.

PRO TIPS

✦ Try repeating this project using different personalities or different balloons.

✦ Make each movie differently and see how much personality you can bring to life with your different choices.

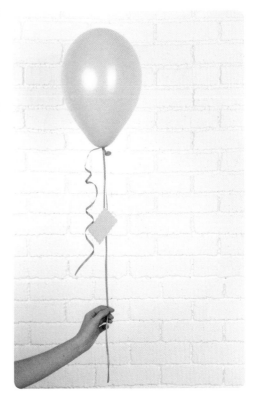

MESSAGE IN A MOVIE

A video greetings card is a great way to send a message to someone who lives far away, or even somebody close by who needs cheering up.

There are two project ideas here for two different types of message. Give them a go and then have a think about what else you can create to send to somebody.

FOR A VIDEO GREETINGS CARD YOU'LL NEED...

- Photos of your recipient

- A scanner/camera (if your photos are printed out)

- A video camera

- Basic video editing software

- Basic photo software

PLAN YOUR GREETING

✦ Think about your message, and who you are sending it to. Think about what kind of sense of humour they have, how they are feeling and what kind of thing would make them smile – these are good indicators of the kind of greeting you should send.

✦ Do some research: try and find some photos or videos of your recipient. If they are printed you'll need to scan them into your computer.

✦ Create an introduction for your message by combining these images in an editing programme.

SHOOT YOUR MESSAGE

✦ Set the camera up to record your message. Make sure there is plenty of light and it's quiet enough for your message to be heard.

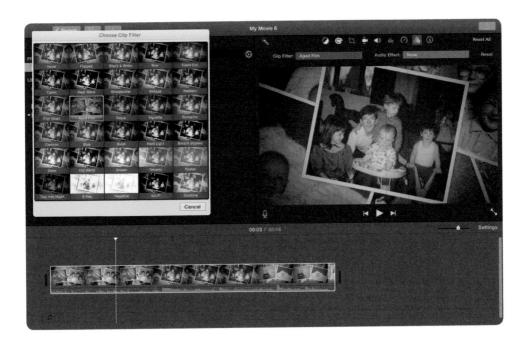

+ Rehearse what you are going to say (thinking about what would make them happy!).

+ Record the message, and retry until you're happy with it.

ASSEMBLE YOUR GREETINGS CARD!

+ Upload your video message.

+ Drag your video message into the project you made earlier in your video editor.

+ Watch it back and check you're happy with it and export your film.

+ Then then all you need to do is send it to your recipient. Check with an adult about the best way to do this: they might have an email address for the person, or be able to help you share your greeting on social media.

TO CREATE A CHRISTMAS CRACKER YOU'LL NEED...

- Some Christmas decorations

- A camera

- A tripod

- Basic editing software

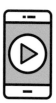

This is a perfect video project for sending holiday greetings to somebody! Learn how to create a heartwarming festive montage and then spice it up with some cheesy cracker jokes!

PLAN YOUR GREETING

✦ Think about your message, and what Christmas means to you and your recipients. How will you create the perfect Christmassy mood?

✦ Think of some great Christmas jokes – the cheesier the better!

SHOOT YOUR CRACKER!

✦ Shoot some **CLOSE-UP** shots of your Christmas decorations. Try to get really close to the objects.

✦ Lots of decorations are shiny and bright. Can you find interesting ways of framing the lights and reflections on the shiny surfaces?

✦ Have a think about other jolly winter images such as cosy fireplaces, snowy hills or stars in the sky to go into your montage. Shoot as many shots as you can think of.

✦ Next, set up a tripod and then turn the camera so it's facing you sitting in a comfortable chair.

✦ Record yourself telling your seasonal jokes to the camera.

✦ Finish with a personal message to whoever you're sending the greeting to.

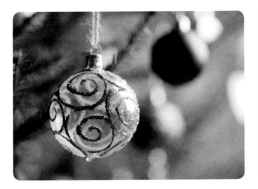

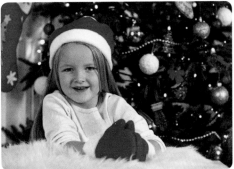

CARDS FOR ALL OCCASIONS

There are lots of video greetings cards that you could create...

- ✦ Record yourself telling some jokes for April Fool's Day!
- ✦ Create a mini horror film for Hallowe'en (see page 124) for ideas).
- ✦ Sing a lullaby for a newborn baby.
- ✦ Send a thank-you message for a present you've received – including footage of you using it.

EDITING YOUR VIDEO GREETING

- ✦ Upload your footage and open your editing package.

- ✦ Drag all your decoration shots into the timeline. Trim off the parts of the shots that you don't want the audience to see.

- ✦ Insert some **FADE TRANSITIONS** between the shots to create a nice flow between the shots (see page 56 for more ideas on this).

- ✦ If you like, you can record yourself singing a seasonal song using the voiceover feature of your editing application. (See page 70 for tips.)

- ✦ Then, add your personal greeting and jokes.

- ✦ Add some cracking noise special effects and a comedy drum-roll sound effect to make your jokes really zing!

- ✦ Watch back your project and check that you are happy with it.

- ✦ In Video Effects you might be able to find a warm effect that will add a nice golden glow to the video clips and help it feel extra cosy.

- ✦ Then export and send the video in the same way as above.

MAKING
PROGRAMMES

Making movies doesn't just have to be about the big screen. There are lots of exciting ways you can put your movie-making skills to use in creating the kind of programmes you see on television or streamed online.

This section is all about people power. You'll learn how a movie maker can help people to tell their stories, whether as part of a news bulletin or in a talk show format. Your filming and editing skills will come together to help you produce professional-style programmes from your own home!

BREAKING NEWS

YOU'LL NEED...

- A camera

- A studio set

- An outdoor location

- Editing software or app

Make a news report and cover a breaking news story live from the scene.

WRITE YOUR STORY

✦ Decide on your topic or theme. Your news report could be serious and linked to your school work, or a comedy made up of silly stories.

✦ Think of a name for your news channel and news reporters too.

✦ Write up your story and do any research you might need.

STORYBOARD

✦ News reports are mostly made up of two shots: one in the news studio with a presenter, and one on location with a correspondent. Often the correspondent 'cuts back' to the studio at the end of their location report and the studio presenter 'signs off' and says goodbye to the audience.

✦ Think about how you would like to show these shots. You might like to use **WIDE SHOTS**, or a Medium/ Mid Shot (from waist height).

✦ Depending on your story, you might also like to include some **CUTAWAYS** that show relevant items (see page 60). For instance, if your report is on a new type of chocolate, it's a good idea to show us the chocolate close up in a Cutaway. So we would see the reporter, then cut to the chocolate, and then cut back to the reporter.

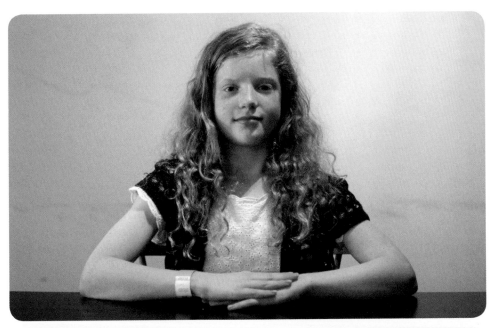

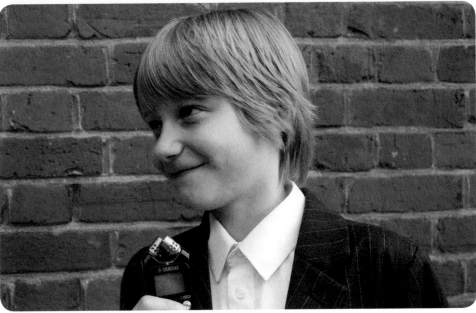

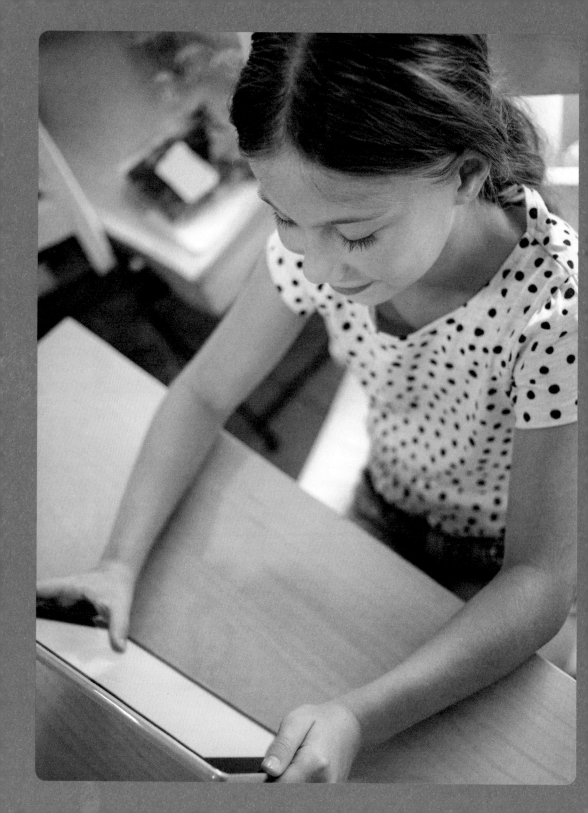

BUILD YOUR SET

+ Using your desk or a table, build yourself a news desk to report from.

+ Think about backgrounds and anything you might like to include in your news studio, such as a lamp or laptop.

SHOOT YOUR FOOTAGE

+ Position your news presenter in the studio set and film them presenting straight to camera.

+ As these are mostly long takes, it's a good idea to rehearse your report first and learn any lines.

+ Once you've finished in the studio, move on to filming your location report with the correspondent. Again, try to rehearse the report so that you are able to film it in one take (without having to stop and start again).

+ Once you've filmed your studio presenter and your correspondent, you're ready to edit.

+ Transfer your footage to your editing programme or app.

EDITING

+ Choose the best takes of your report to sequence in your movie.

+ First include the studio reporter, and then cut to the correspondent.

+ Include any Cutaways within the correspondent section, splitting the clip to sequence the Cutaways in between.

+ At the end of the correspondent report, cut back to the studio presenter to sign off.

+ Include an introductory news title with a catchy jingle. Many programmes offer this option, or you can build your own using a title screen and sound effects.

+ Add in 'ticker' text featuring other news stories along the bottom of your report to make it look convincing.

ANIMAL CAM

YOU'LL NEED...

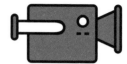

- A camera

Nature documentaries are some of the most amazing and popular programmes there are. This project is a great way to make a film about animals, filming the world from their point of view. Show your audience what your pet dog sees, or how it feels to be a tiny ant scurrying along the floor.

✦ First of all, pick an animal to represent. Have a good think about how it moves and how tall it is. If you have any pets at home, watch them moving around. Or if your animal can be found in the wild, try to find out how it behaves from videos or a trip to the zoo.

✦ Once you've got a good idea of how this animal moves around, hold your camera in the right position. Try to position your camera at the level of the animal's eyes. For instance, if your animal is an insect, place yourself and your camera low down on the floor and angle the camera looking up. If your animal is tall, like a giraffe, think about using a tripod to get the camera high enough to look down on the world. Remember, you're not aiming to film the animal's face, but what this animal would see. Think of the camera as their eyes.

✦ While recording, try to copy the movements that the animal would make. Travel around your location, moving the camera as your animal.

PRO TIPS

✦ Ask a friend to be an actor and interact with the camera. Perhaps they can give your dog a biscuit, or run away from your fearsome tiger. Ask your actor to look directly at the camera.

✦ Shoot a range of animals for your movie collection. Ask your friends if they can guess which animal's point of view you've created in your own Animal Cam quiz.

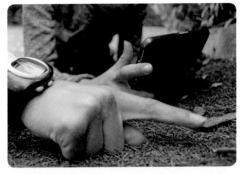

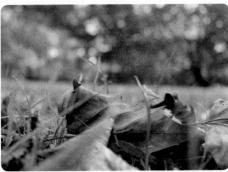

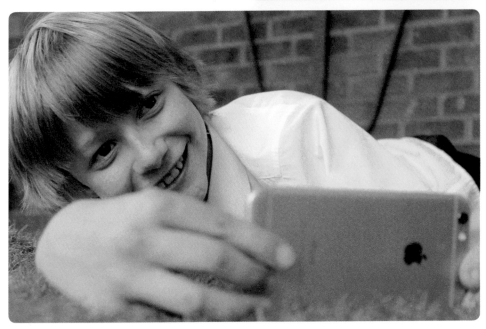

VOX POP

YOU'LL NEED...

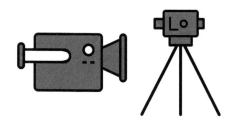

- A camera

- A tripod

- A group of friends, family members or volunteers!

- Basic editing software

A **VOX POP** is a great method of presenting lots of people's ideas or opinions. It shows a lot of people answering a question, and the footage is edited together into a very quick sequence that feels lively and entertaining when you watch it.

This can be a fun way to do research into a topic – or to find out which football team is the best, what your classmates would do if they won the lottery, or which superpower your family would most like to have! It also works well as part of a talk show (see page 102) or a news report (page 92).

WRITE YOUR QUESTIONS

✦ Think of a list of questions. Try to come up with a few different examples: you might have some silly questions, and then a few more serious ones so you have something to experiment with when you start editing.

✦ Look at your questions and decide on an order in which to ask them. If you have some silly ones, put these first as a warm-up. Asking something tricky without a practice question can catch people off guard!

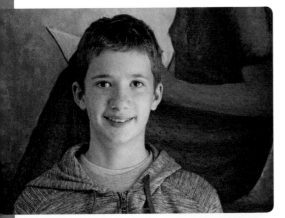
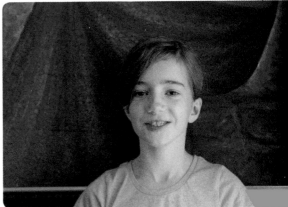
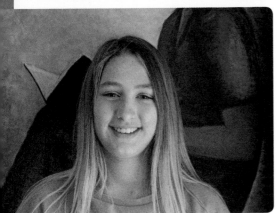
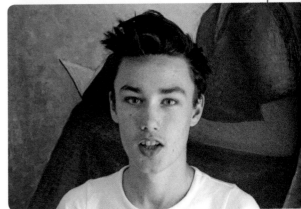

SET UP YOUR SHOT

✦ Choose somewhere with lots of light and an interesting background.

✦ You might want to choose somewhere that reflects the question you're asking. For example, if you are asking a question about the environment you could pick an outdoor location.

SHOOT YOUR VOX POP

✦ Invite your first guest to stand in front of your chosen backdrop.

✦ Aim to shoot a **MID SHOT**. This will mean that there is space in the shot for them to move their hands or head when they're talking.

✦ Use a tripod to make sure the shot stays the same for each person.

✦ Stand slightly to the side of the camera, and ask your guest to look you in the eyes when they are speaking. This will mean they show the camera their face, without staring down the lens.

✦ Press Record and then ask your guest the questions.

✦ If your guest gets tongue-tied, reshoot until you're happy with it.

✦ Then, thank your guest and ask for the next one. Ask exactly the same questions in the same order.

✦ Repeat until you've done everyone – you can of course film yourself too if you want to join in.

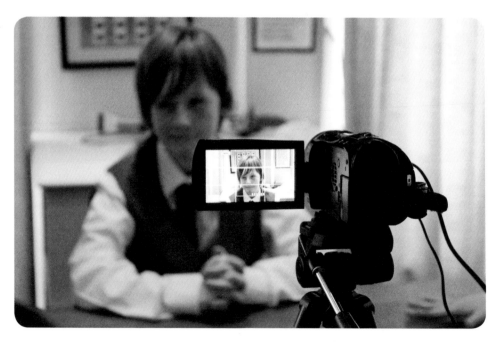

EDITING

+ Open your editing software and upload your footage.

+ Watch it back, and see which question provokes the most interesting answers. This will be your main question.

+ Assemble your footage so you can only hear the answer to the main question. For now, get rid of any other footage. You should have a sequence of lots of clips that are only a few seconds long.

+ Watch it back, and see what you think of the rhythm. There might be a string of shots that cut into each other really quickly. Then there might be a few sections where people take longer to answer, and so the clips are longer and the film seems slower.

+ Experiment with changing the order so the footage flows in an interesting way. You might have a string of people saying the same one-word answer and then interrupt this with a funny answer that will surprise your audience. Keep experimenting until you're happy with the rhythm.

+ Now, create a title that displays the question that everyone answers. You can either have it as a standalone title before your film begins, or as something that runs across the bottom of each clip.

+ If you're happy with your question, move onto the next one and repeat the process until you have a string of vox pops.

+ If you like, you can add music underneath your interviews. Make sure the music isn't so loud as to make it hard to hear the answers. You may need to turn the volume up on some of the clips too.

MAKE A GAME OF IT

You could make a fun game with vox pops. Film and edit a series of vox pops, but don't add a title to explain what the question is. See if people can guess what question you asked!

MAKE YOUR OWN TALK SHOW

YOU'LL NEED...

- A camera
- Some interesting friends or family
- A talk show style set
- Editing programme or app

Interview your friends and make your own fun talk show.

Encourage them to tell any interesting secrets or stories, ask about their ambitions, favourite hobbies or recent holidays, or find out how they would change the world if they were in charge for one day.

WRITE YOUR QUESTIONS

✦ Decide on your interview topic and write up a list of related questions to ask your friends.

✦ Try to choose interesting questions that will tell your audience something they don't already know.

✦ Also think about any **PIECE TO CAMERA** sections, where the host can talk directly to the audience through the camera. These make good introductions and 'sign-offs', where the host says goodbye to the audience at the end.

STORYBOARD

✦ Plan out your shots and think about what you would like to include.

✦ Consider using a wide **ESTABLISHING SHOT**, as well as individual **CLOSE-UPS**, or some **OVER THE SHOULDER SHOTS**.

✦ **CUTAWAYS** can be useful for holidays or hobbies, so think of any extra footage or images you might want to use and don't forget your Piece to Camera sections.

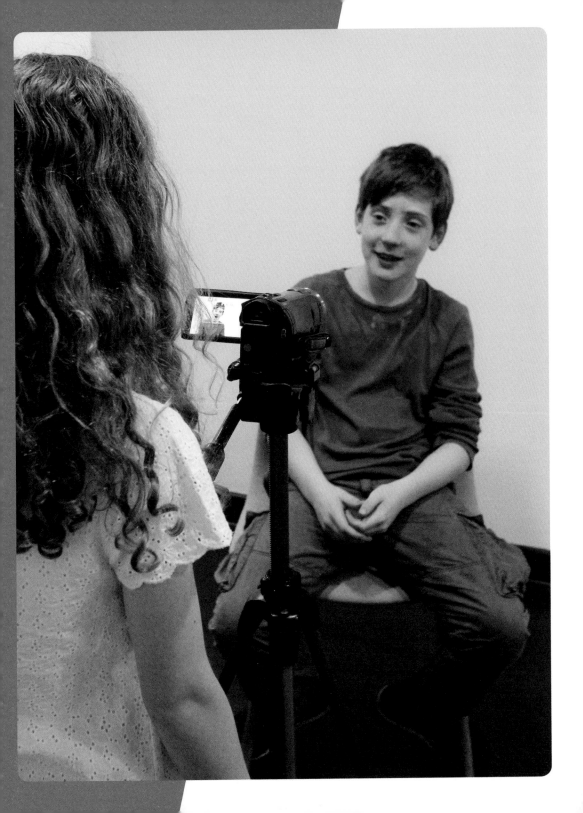

CASTING AND COSTUME

✦ Cast your friends in your talk show and invite them over.

✦ Decide if you want one of them to be the host, or the interviewer. If you plan to be the host, think about who can help you on the crew as your camera operator.

✦ Also consider if you would like them to wear any specific costume, or to bring any props along. For instance, if their interview is about ice skating, ask them to bring their skates.

BUILD YOUR SET

✦ Find a location for your talk show. This could be your bedroom, on the sofa in your living room, or perhaps cushions or beanbags in the garden.

✦ Choose a set that works for your talk show and use decorations to give it a unique design.

SHOOT YOUR FOOTAGE

✦ Shoot your talk show following your storyboard.

✦ Prepare your friends for the shots and angles that you've chosen. They may need to repeat their answers several times to make sure you get the right shots.

✦ Make sure they talk to the host and not to camera so that you get natural on-screen performances.

EDITING

✦ Transfer your footage to your editing programme or app.

✦ Choose the clips that you want to include and sequence them in your movie.

✦ Cut very carefully to ensure continuity between your different shots and watch out for repetition or jumps in the speech.

✦ Try to make each cut as smooth as possible between your shots and clips.

✦ Once you've sequenced your clips, add in a fun title screen introducing your talk show, and add end credits along with some music to finish off your video.

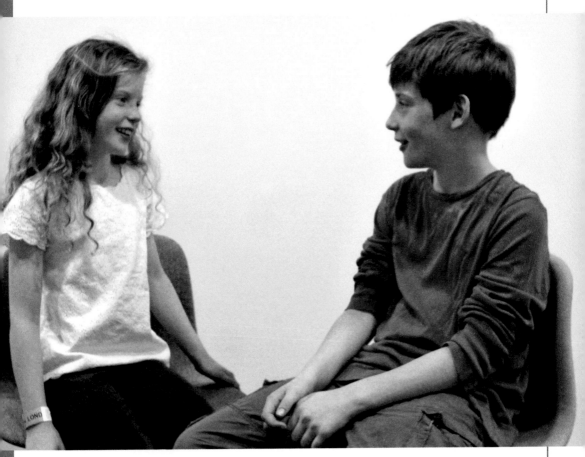

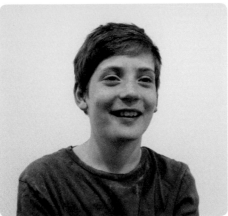

PRO TIPS

✦ Try making weekly episodes of your talk show featuring different friends, or interviewing them on different topics.
✦ Talk shows are great features for vlogs and can make a fun long-term project.

MOVIE-
MAKING
STORIES

So now you're a pro when it comes to scriptwriting, filming and editing – are you ready to make a blockbuster?

Many movies can be put into categories called 'genres' (pronounced 'jon-ra') depending on the kind of story they tell: comedies, horror movies, spy films and so on. Different genres have different styles of movie-making, and in this section you'll have a chance to explore a few of the most popular.

Do you fancy turning your friends into superheroes or scaring them silly with some spooky surprises? Maybe you'd like to create suspense and mystery in a spy story, or turn the clock back to create a classic old movie. The projects in this section take you through all the steps needed to make your own movie masterpieces, with plenty of scope for your own ideas and creativity.

So what are you waiting for – it's time to get shooting on your own big-screen smash!

SHOOTING SUPERHEROES

This project shows lots of different ways to turn an ordinary friend into an extraordinary superhero. Try the different techniques individually, or put them together to make a superpower montage!

FOR SUPERSONIC SPEED YOU'LL NEED...

- A camera
- A tripod
- An actor
- Editing software or app

The best location for this scene is a park or garden where you have lots of space, so that you can film your actors standing very far away from the camera (this is called an **EXTREME WIDE SHOT**).

- ✦ Film a shot of your actor standing near the camera and then running far away (but still in shot) and back again. Ask them to finish by standing still at the front of the shot, and get them to do a few laps. The longer the run the better, but make sure that they stay in shot at all times.

- ✦ Transfer your footage to your editing programme. Select the parts of the clip where they are running. You might find it helpful to cut your footage into separate sections: clips where they are running, and clips where they are standing still.

- ✦ Using the retiming tool, speed up the running sections. Keep the standing still sections at normal speed.

- ✦ Add some whooshing sound effects to emphasis their super speed! Think about making your own super speed sound effects using foley (see page 72).

FOR FLYING YOU'LL NEED...

- A green sheet or green wall

- An actor (make sure your actor isn't wearing any green coloured clothing)

- A camera

- A tripod

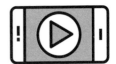

- Editing software or app

If your editing programme includes a green-screen effect, you can use this to make it appear as though your characters are flying. Green screening, or Chroma Key, works by removing the green colour from your shot, so that you can replace it with another background.

✦ Position your camera so that it is facing the green backdrop. Your green backdrop should be as flat a colour as possible, without any shadows. If you're using a sheet, try to hang it tightly so it doesn't have too many wrinkles. You may want to use a lamp to help fill in any dark patches.

✦ Make sure that the camera can't see anything behind or next to the green, and that the green fills the shot. Ask your actor to stand in front of the green (you can also use a toy or other prop to stand in for an actor).

✦ Ask your actor to position themselves so that they look as if they are flying, leaning forward. Frame the shot so we cannot see their feet standing on the floor.

✦ Film your actor flying against the green backdrop. Try to film for at least a minute so that you have plenty of footage.

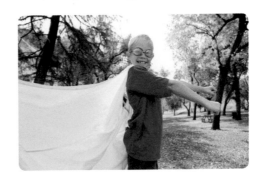

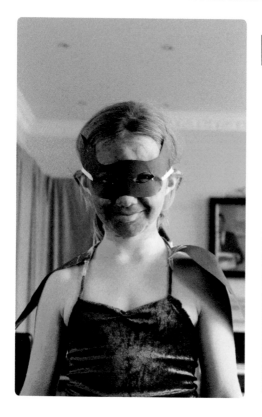

PRO TIPS

✦ Be very careful not to give away that your actor is standing up. For an added effect you could use a fan to make it look like their hair is blowing in the wind.

✦ If your background doesn't completely vanish, experiment with the colour settings to make all of the colours a little more green.

✦ Experiment with your sky shots to see which ones look most effective. Find some air rushing sound effects (or record your own using foley) and you're up, up and away!

✦ Now, shoot some footage of the sky. Be careful not to point your camera directly at the sun. Film various shots of the sky so you can experiment with them later. Shoot at least one **TRACKING SHOT** so that you have some movement in the sequence.

✦ Transfer your footage to your editing programme. Sequence your footage and follow the guidance in your programme to add in your clips for the green-screen effect.

Usually, you add your background images or video first, and then layer the green-screen footage over the top.

✦ Once your clips are in sequence, apply a Chroma Key effect (sometimes called Keyer or Green Screen) to the green screen clips to erase the green background. You should now see that your actor is a flying superhero!

FOR INVISIBILITY YOU'LL NEED...

- An actor with some green and non-green clothing

- A green cloth or sheet

- A camera

- A tripod

- Editing programme or app

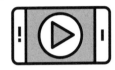

This green-screen effect is easy, but incredibly effective. It creates an 'invisibility cloak' that can be used to make superheroes disappear.

✦ Find a filming location that doesn't have anything green it.

✦ Ask your actor to wear some clothes that aren't green. If they have green eyes, ask them to wear dark glasses.

✦ To make this effect work properly you will need to make sure the camera stays really still. Use a tripod or something else to hold the camera really steady for every shot you take. Set a **WIDE SHOT** so that we can see the background, the cloth and the actor.

✦ Ask your actor to enter the shot, then pick up the green cloth, cover themselves with it like a cloak, and do something that you might do

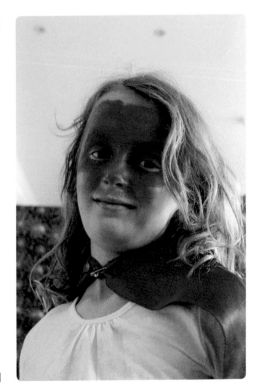

with an invisibility cloak. Maybe they'll use their invisibility to steal something, spy on somebody, or to put a superhero device in a key place. Rehearse this carefully so that your actor is confident. When you're finished, everything covered by the cloth will turn invisible!

✦ Being very careful not to move the camera or change the angle or the zoom, ask your actor to leave the shot. Film the background without your actor in the scene. It needs to be exactly the same, just without the actor and cloth.

✦ Transfer your footage to your editing programme or app. Following the guidance in your programme, layer the Wide Shot with your actor on top of the background shot. Apply the Chroma Key or green-screen effect. Your cloak and everything covered by it should now vanish!

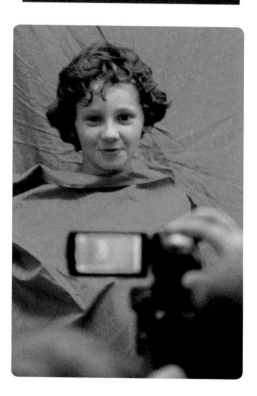

FOR TELEKENESIS YOU'LL NEED...

- A prop that you can throw (without risk of breaking it)

- A camera

- Editing software or app

- An actor

~~~~~~

This technique creates the impression that your superhero can move things with their mind (telekinesis).

✦ Set up a shot that shows the floor and your actor.

✦ Ask your actor to throw the prop on to the floor. Ask them to throw it with an open hand with their fingers outstretched. Once they've let go of the prop they should keep their hand open and reaching towards the object.

✦ Film the shot using a **WIDE SHOT**.

✦ Film a **CLOSE-UP** shot of your actor's face looking like they are concentrating.

✦ Transfer the footage into your editing software.

✦ Select the throwing shot, and then reverse the clip. It should now look as though the actor is magically making the object fly into their hand. You could also use the retiming function to slow or speed up the footage to make the movement look more supernatural. Insert the Close-up of their face into the scene for added detail.

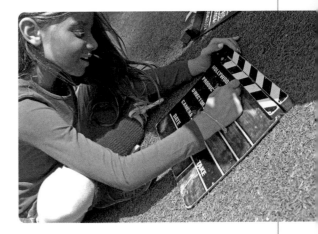

GO BACK IN TIME: MAKE AN OLD MOVIE

YOU'LL NEED...

- A camera

- Actors and a set

- Costumes and props

- Video footage

- Editing software or an editing app

- Piano music audio file (.mp3 or similar)

In this project, you'll create a movie comedy that looks as if it's from the early days of cinema. At that time, movies were silent, filmed in black and white, and a pianist would have played a live soundtrack in the cinema. Comedies were popular, particularly slapstick physical comedies in the style of Charlie Chaplin or Buster Keaton.

STORYBOARD AND SHOOT YOUR FOOTAGE

✦ First, draw up a storyboard for your comedy. Think about which shots will best show your comedy elements.

✦ Remember it's silent, so **CLOSE UPS** and **WIDE SHOTS** can be helpful at giving your audience clues about what's happening in your story.

✦ Consider including some classic slapstick tricks including falling over a banana skin or a cops-and-robbers chase scene.

✦ Once you've filmed your shots, you're ready to edit! Transfer your footage to your editing programme or app.

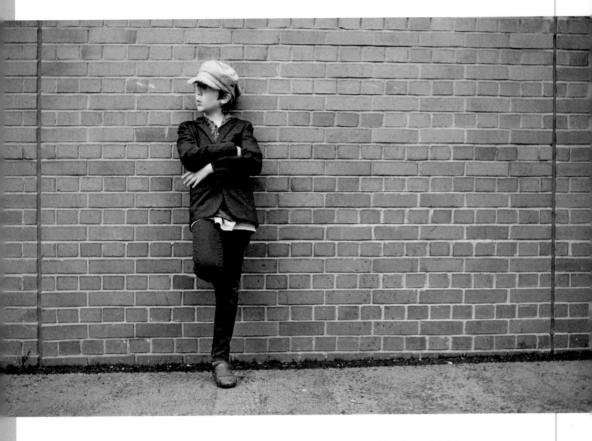

SEQUENCE YOUR SHOTS

✦ First, sequence your shots in your editing programme or app.

✦ Choose which clips you want to include from your footage and order them as you want them to appear.

ADD IN VIDEO EFFECTS

✦ Once you have your footage sequenced, add in some video effects to send it back in time.

✦ Choose a Black and White (sometimes called Mono) effect to give it an old movie appearance.

✦ You can also try Sepia, Aged Films or Film Grain effects to give it an authentic feel.

✦ Make sure you apply this effect to each of your clips so that your film looks consistent all the way through.

✦ **ADD A SOUNDTRACK**
Choose a piece of piano music to score your movie. You may even want to record your own.

✦ Add the music to your clips and mute the video footage.

ADD TITLES

✦ Give your movie a title and add an opening title screen to the beginning.

✦ Titles from this time period featured white writing on a black background.

✦ Choose an old-fashioned style script font for a realistic effect.

✦ You might also want to include some title screens featuring key lines of dialogue from your characters. As we can't hear them speak, it can be helpful to include titles.

✦ Add these in at the relevant story points, keeping to the same style as your title screen.

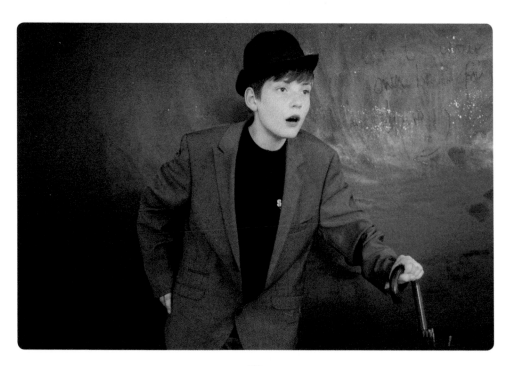

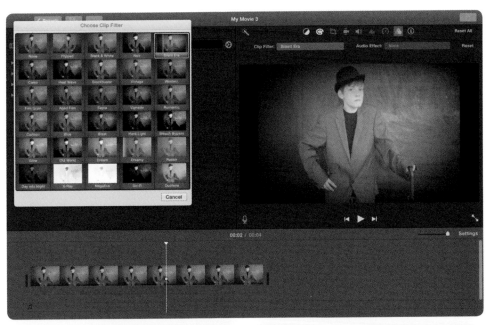

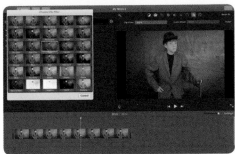

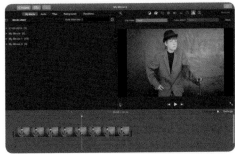

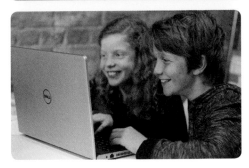

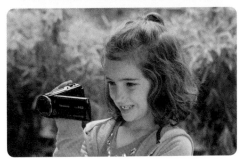

HOW TO MAKE A SPY MOVIE

YOU'LL NEED...

- A camera
- A tripod
- Actors
- Costumes and props
- Editing software

~~~~~~

Everybody has a favourite spy movie. They are fantastic fun and a good challenge in building suspense and developing your storytelling skills. In this project, you will create your own mystery story and keep your audience on the edge of their seat.

WRITE YOUR STORY

✦ First, have a think about your story. Starting with a character is often helpful; work through the Create Cracking Characters project on page 32 to come up with an interesting spy, detective, or villain to base your movie on. Think about whether your character belongs to a bigger agency, or if they are a sole agent working alone.

✦ Next, give your character a mystery to solve. This could involve inventing a nemesis character for them, or it could be a set of mysterious circumstances. Perhaps somebody has disappeared, or perhaps they've intercepted a warning from the rival side. Maybe there is a crime to solve.

✦ Consider the clues you can plant for your spy along the way... What happens that leads them to solve the mystery?

✦ Think of a 'red herring' or a twist that you can include to keep things interesting. A 'red herring' is a false piece of information,

PRO TIPS

✦ Include a dramatic chase
  sequence with lots of quick
  cut, pacy edits. Try to use some
  high and low angles here to
  add drama to the sequence and
  make your audience believe
  your characters are chasing in
  some dangerous locations.

✦ Think about using some
  chroma key special effects,
  such as explosions or laser
  beams. You can source lots of
  free special effects that use
  green screen techniques and
  can be applied to your movie
  projects.

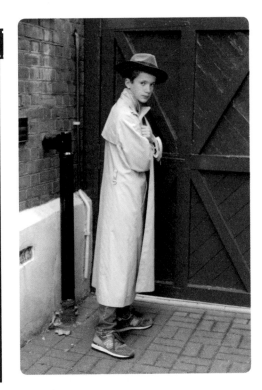

designed to trick your audience
into seeing something untrue. If
you can include a few surprising
plot twists, this will help keep your
audience guessing.

✦ Include some danger! You need
  to make the adventure dangerous
  for your spy. A strong villain can
  do this, or consider including a
  treacherous environment. If your
  spy is part of a bigger agency,
  think about including some double
  agents who can double-cross
  your spy.

PRE-PRODUCTION

✦ Once you have your story, draw
  out your storyboard shot by
  shot, thinking about which shot
  types and angles you would like
  to include. Think carefully about
  any important details, especially
  regarding the clues. You might
  want to show these in **CLOSE-
  UPS,** to make it clear to your
  audience what the clue is. **TILT
  SHOTS, POINT OF VIEW SHOTS**
  and **EXTREME CLOSE-UPS** can
  help add an air of mystery and
  build suspense. **HIGH ANGLES,**

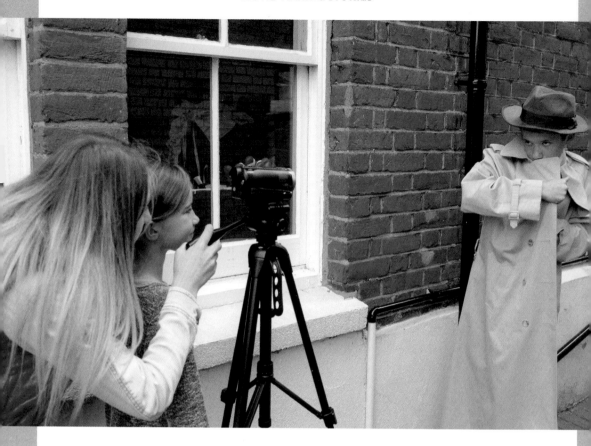

LOW ANGLES and **DUTCH** (or **CANTED**) **ANGLES** can also work well to create the impression of heights, scaling tall buildings, or falling. You might also want to show your villain from a Low Angle, so that they appear impressive and powerful.

✦ Cast your movie. Decide who you will need to act in your video. Think about which of your friends you

would like to perform, and whether you would also like your family to join in.

✦ Decide what your characters should wear as costume, and think about any props they might need. It might be helpful to make a list, scene by scene. Costume can play a huge part in a spy movie, as it tells us a lot about their character. Is your spy suave in a suit and bow tie, or perhaps they are traditional in a trench coat and trilby hat? Talk to your actors about their props and costume, and see if they can contribute any items that will help in your shoot.

✦ Think about your locations, and any places you can use to shoot your movie. Make sure you have permission to film in each of these places.

✦ Schedule your shoot. Make sure your performers are all available at the same time and know where to go for your shoot. Sometimes writing up a 'Call Sheet' (or an official schedule) for everyone can help to organise your team.

PRODUCTION

✦ Rehearse with your performers carefully to make sure everyone understands what you need from each shot. If you have written a script, make sure you give your actors plenty of time to learn their lines and to rehearse!

✦ Shoot through your storyboard shot by shot.

PRO TIPS

✦ Think carefully about your characterisation and see if you can find ways of incorporating character traits or flaws into your story (see page 35).

✦ Write a script for your actors. Work through the Sizzling Scripts project on page 36.

✦ Log your shots. While shooting your movie, make a note of which are your favourite takes and why. This will make it much easier to find them when you come to edit.

✦ There are lots of visual styles you can adopt for a spy movie. Experiment with colour and soundtrack to give your movie a distinctive feel. Black and White effect along with some jazz music for example, or experiment with bright colour effects to introduce a comic-book style.

✦ Try to watch back some of your footage as you go to make sure you're happy with the production shots. It's not always possible to come back and re-shoot takes another time, so make sure you're happy with the footage on the day.

POST-PRODUCTION

✦ Transfer your footage into your editing programme or app.

✦ Working scene by scene, select and sequence the clips you want to show in your movie, choosing the best takes. Remember to follow your storyboard closely, to make sure you include all the detail about the clues and characters.

✦ Add in any **TRANSITIONS** you think will help to tell your story. Spy movies can include slow transitions, such as **FADES** or **DISSOLVES**, along with quick **STRAIGHT CUTS** in moments of high action. Choose your transitions to reflect the pace of the story at that time.

✦ Choose your soundtrack. Add in music and sound effects that will help to tell your story and give your movie atmosphere, pace and rhythm. Sound effects can help to enhance the mystery, especially if the sound happens 'off screen' and your audience can't see what created it.

✦ Consider any visual effects you might like to apply. Experiment with different tones to see if you can create some extra atmosphere.

✦ Add titles into your movie. An opening title and a credit sequence detailing your actors and your crew will help your movie to look like a professional production.

✦ When you are ready, export and share your spy movie!

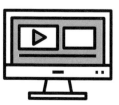

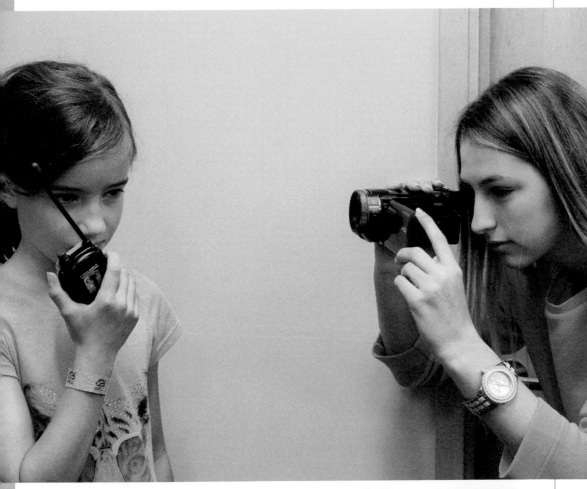

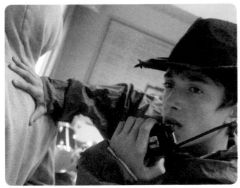

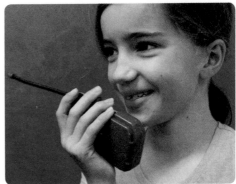

AARRGGHH! MAKE YOUR OWN HORROR MOVIE!

Whether it's Hallowe'en, or you just have a brilliant idea for a ghost story, scary films are really fun to make. This project uses a few techniques and ingredients that will make your films look super spooky.

Before you start shooting, have a think about your story. Perhaps it is a supernatural story about a monster, or a ghost. It could also be more realistic – perhaps somebody locked into their home alone.

Once you've got your idea, have a read through these examples to help you shoot something really effective. Once you have your story idea, storyboard and shoot your movie and then edit it with some scary music and sound effects.

FOR OFF-SCREEN MONSTERS, YOU'LL NEED...

- An actor

- A camera

- A lamp

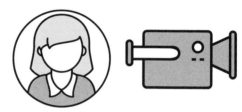

Off-screen monsters can sometimes be scarier than those we see. The audience's imagination will fill in the gaps for you. If you want to create a monster, but don't have a perfect costume, this is a great technique to include in your movie.

For this exercise, shoot a sequence with an actor running away from a monster in three shots.

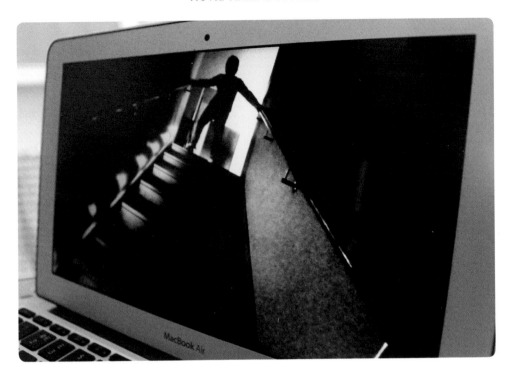

You should be inside for this sequence, as you are going to need to make a shadow using the lamp. A dark room is ideal.

✦ For the first shot, shoot a **POINT OF VIEW SHOT** from the monster's point of view. Hold the camera above your head so that the monster is really tall. Point it down towards the actor in a **HIGH ANGLE** and have them run away from you. Follow them as they run away. Ask them to look at the camera as if it is a monster's face. As you move the camera, think

about how your monster would move. You might be able to mimic their movements through your camera. Ask your actor to play their most terrified expressions.

✦ For the next shot, shoot a reaction shot in a **CLOSE-UP**. Shoot your actor's face as they gaze up at the monster. This time, you should hold the camera really steadily and in front of your actor. This means your audience can tell the difference from your Point of View shot.

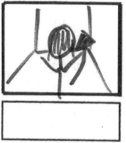 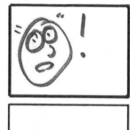 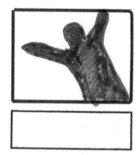

✦ For the third shot, create a scary shadow of the monster. Find some interesting props or cut a monster's outline from a piece of cardboard. Use your imagination to create something really scary. Turn on your lamp and then turn off the rest of the lights of the room. Experiment with the best positions in the room to cast a shadow on a wall using your monster.

✦ Next, find a way to position the camera so that you can't see the props or the lamp, but have a great shot of the shadow. Film the shadow moving slowly and menacingly downwards.

✦ Transfer all your shots to your editing software and sequence them to make your movie. After you've inserted the first shot, insert a bit of the second shot, and then a bit of the third shot. Repeat this pattern, cutting between the three different shots.

✦ Add in some creepy music and sound effects, such as booming monster footprints or breathing.

✦ Watch it back. It should look like the actor is reacting to the shadow that's descending on them. For a really dramatic ending you could then insert a sudden black screen and record a voiceover of the actor screaming. The audience can imagine what happens next!

FOR SILHOUETTES, YOU'LL NEED...

- A very bright background
- A camera
- An actor

This is a great way to show a terrifying character, while also creating an air of mystery around them. Have fun experimenting with it and add it to your other clips.

✦ To create a silhouette, find a really bright background. The plainer this is the better: a white blind over a sunny window is perfect. The plain background will help your silhouette stand out.

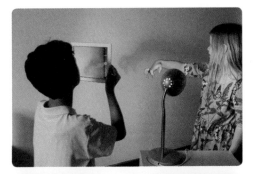

✦ Position your camera so that your actor is standing directly in front of the bright background, and the actor's outline is blacked out against the light. You may want to find a lamp to add some extra light behind the camera. Point the lamp in the direction of the camera but make sure it isn't visible in shot.

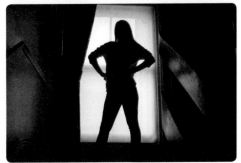

✦ Ask your actor to strike a pose that makes an interesting and scary silhouette. Stretched-out arms, or hands on hips or even an interestingly shaped hat will help to add definition to the shape.

✦ Film your actor's silhouette moving against the background.

CANTED ANGLES AND EXTREME CLOSE-UPS

✦ Horror films are full of shots that show terrified-looking eyes filling the entire screen.

✦ Try to include at least one Extreme Close-up in your movie. When your characters are scared, your audience will be too.

✦ Experiment with including a Canted Angle (sometimes called a Dutch Angle) in your film. Shots on Canted Angles make things look crooked, so they work perfectly to show a creepy monster, or a confused and scared victim. To film a Canted Angle, turn your camera slightly to one side so that the floor and ceiling are uneven in your shot (see page 48).

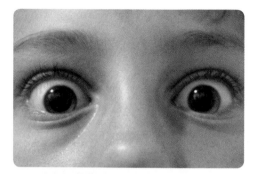

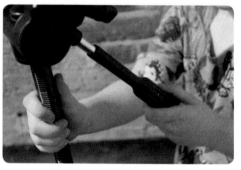

PRO TIPS

✦ Try combining a Canted Angle shot with a silhouette to make something really creepy.

✦ When framing your Extreme Close-ups, try to position your camera very close to your subject rather than relying on the zoom. This will ensure your image quality stays really sharp.

FOR FAKE BLOOD, YOU'LL NEED...

- A bowl
- A teaspoon
- Golden syrup
- Cold water
- Red food colouring
- Blue food colouring
- A sieve
- Cornflour

This recipe is for home-made fake blood that can be made out of things you can find in your kitchen. Using fake blood can help you achieve some fun and gory effects to make your horror movie extra gruesome.

✦ Put three teaspoons of golden syrup and one teaspoon of water in a bowl and mix well.

✦ Add three drops of red food colouring. The mixture should now be a bit thinner and also bright red.

✦ Add a very small drop of blue food colouring. This will make the colour look more like realistic blood.

✦ Add one teaspoon of sifted cornflour to the mixture. Mix this in really well so you don't get any crusty lumps! This should help thicken the mixture slightly.

✦ Leave your fake blood to one side for about ten minutes to let it settle. Have a look at the colour, and add more red if it's looking a bit too dark. Be careful when adding more blue as a little goes a very long way.

✦ Now your blood is ready you can make up your actors. As it's made of edible things it can even go in their mouths. Check with an adult in case of any allergies and be careful not to stain clothes or furniture.

SHARE YOUR MOVIES

Now you're a fully fledged movie maker, you can share your movies with an audience.

Host your own premiere events and invite friends and family to watch your hard work on screen. Connect your camera or editing device to your television screen, or play your movies through an online channel.

You can also put your movies onto DVD to send to family members and friends. You can even design your own labels.

Why not encourage your friends to make movies too and then start your own festival or awards ceremony?

Make sure there is plenty of popcorn and enjoy watching your movies!

EXPORTING YOUR MOVIES

When you are ready to share your movies, you need to export them from your editing programme or app. Depending on your device, you may be able to export or share your movies straight to YouTube or social media apps. Or it may be a slightly longer process, particularly when working on advanced editing programmes.

Before you export any of your movies, check out our tips for sharing safely on page 137.

✦ The simplest way to export is to turn your movie into a file, following guidance on your programme or app.

✦ There are several types of movie files, but the most versatile ones are: .mov, .mp4 or .avi.

✦ Try to export your movies as one of these file types, so that you can share them online and also on DVD.

✦ You will find lots of settings if you are exporting your movies manually. Unless you are confident in changing these, try to keep to the automatic settings.

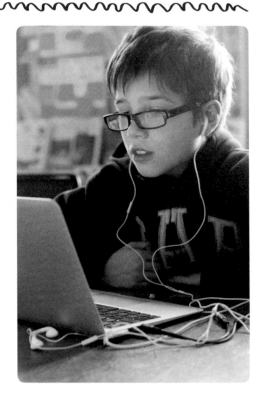

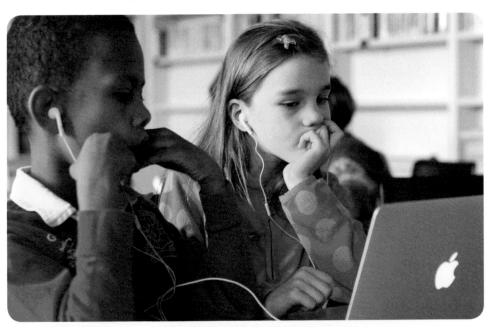

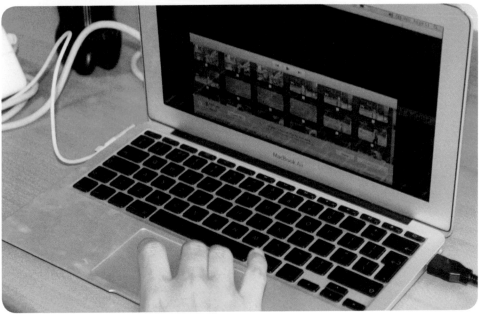

HOST YOUR OWN PREMIERE EVENT

Professional movie makers often celebrate their movies with official 'premieres'. This is the first time the finished movie is shown to anybody other than the cast and crew. Depending on the scale of the movie, this might be a big, glamorous red-carpet event, or it could be a screening at a film festival, where several films are presented together.

With a little planning, you can launch your movie at a premiere or festival presentation at home. Follow the steps below to organise your own fantastic event to share your own movies.

✦ Decide on which movies you want to show. It may be one movie, or a collection that you've made. You can even invite fellow movie-making friends to join in with their movies too.

✦ Decide on the day and time. Give yourself plenty of time to get ready and prepare. Make sure you get permission from a parent or carer to host your premiere.

✦ Invite your guests: family members and friends, especially friends who also love making movies! Tell them the time, date and place.

✦ Make sure you have your movies finished and ready to show. Test your playback connection in advance, so you can be sure of everything working perfectly on your big day.

✦ Decorate! You can make some posters to promote your movies, or add some balloons for a celebratory touch. You could even include your own red carpet.

✦ Think about any extra information you might want to give your guests. Prepare some programmes that explain your movies' plots and the process of making them.

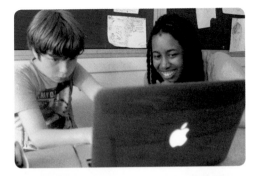

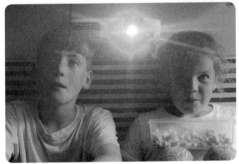

PRO TIPS

✦ Make your event extra special and ask everybody to dress up in glamorous 'red carpet' outfits.

✦ Ask a parent or relative to be your papparazzi and take pictures of your premiere event.

✦ If you're including other movie makers in your event, you can add an awards ceremony to make it even more celebratory. You can give serious category awards such as 'Best Acting Performance' or 'Best Camera Work', or be playful and include awards such as 'Best Bloopers'.

✦ Write a speech to introduce your movies and to thank everyone for coming. If you can learn it, or use cue cards rather than reading it out, then you're on your way to becoming a professional movie maker.

✦ Make some popcorn (or other refreshments) ready for when your guests arrive.

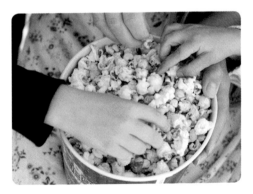

✦ Welcome your guests and deliver your speech.

✦ Watch and enjoy your movies!

SETTING UP AN ONLINE CHANNEL

You can share your movies with others around the world through your own video channel. It's easy to set one up and to update it whenever you make a new movie. Your channel will be dedicated entirely to your movies.

The most popular place to set up your channel is on YouTube, at www.youtube.com, although you can also use Vimeo, at www.vimeo.com, or a social media account to publish your movies.

✦ Whenever you make a new movie, publish it on your channel so that others can see your latest projects.

✦ Include a description of your movie and adjust the settings to suit your preferences.

✦ Your channel can be exclusive to those you personally invite, or it can be public for everyone to see.

✦ Sharing your movies publicly can help to grow your audience, but going public also comes with responsibilities.

✦ Make sure you follow our tips for safe sharing (see opposite page).

We work with young movie makers all around the world, and we would love to see your movies!

You can share your work with us and with other young movie makers online in our Video Gallery.

Visit www.sparks-ignite.com/tmmb and enter your video details.

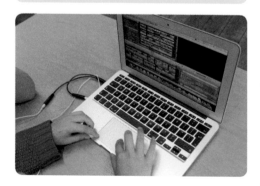

SAFE SHARING ONLINE

Follow these tips to make sure you're sharing your movies safely.

✦ Make sure you have a parent or carer's permission to share your movies online.

✦ If you include your friends in your movies, check for permission with each of them and their parents before publishing online.

✦ Consider making your channel private, or 'unlisting' your movies so that only the people you invite can watch them. If using a social media platform, consider making your account private so that you authorise your followers.

✦ Don't publish any personal details on your channel and avoid including personal details in your movies. For instance, only include the first names of you or your friends, and don't reveal the name of your street or your school in your movies.

✦ Consider turning off the Comments feature on your channel to safeguard against any inappropriate comments.

✦ If you choose to enable Comments, ask a parent or carer to help in setting up a search term filter. Add words and phrases to your 'black list' to prevent inappropriate postings. Visit www.support.google.com for more information.

EQUIPMENT GUIDE

All the projects in this book can be done with any camera equipment you have to hand at home. You don't need a high-tech camera to be able to achieve fantastic movie-making results with these projects.

YOU CAN SHOOT ANY OF OUR PROJECTS ON A...

- Camcorder

- Mobile phone camera

- Tablet camera

- The video mode of a digital camera

- Anything else with a video shooting mode

TECHNICAL SPECIFICATIONS HD stands for High Definition, and offers higher image quality than cameras that use SD (standard definition).

4K or UHD (ultra HD) is a newer format than HD and offers a much higher picture quality, but it is much more expensive and also produces very large computer files. HD should look great for any of the projects in this book.

AUDIO Most camcorders include an internal microphone. If a camera specifies external audio this means that you can plug an external microphone into the camera to enhance your sound recordings. If this is the case, check it also has an internal microphone too.

SD CARDS Most camcorders or photographic camcorders record onto SD cards (although some can record onto an internal hard drive). As HD video can make fairly large files you should aim for a card that's at least 8GB in size so you have plenty of room for your masterpieces.

TRIPODS You should aim for a tripod that is light enough to carry around on set, and has a range of height adjustments. Your tripod will probably have ways to extend or shorten the legs, as well as a handle to pan, tilt, and cant the camera to get the perfect shot. Although not essential for filming, it is a very handy piece of movie-making kit. Most tripods will fit most camcorders and cameras, though you may need a special adapter to fit your tablet or phone.

REFLECTOR A reflector board is a great way to bounce light into a shot without needing to plug in a lamp. Most will come with a variety of colour surfaces: the white side will bounce light into the shot, the silver will bounce even more light into the shot, the gold will make the light look warm (perfect for a fashion shoot) and the black will make the shot look darker by absorbing the light.

GREEN SCREEN There are a variety of types available, with the most simple looking like a green bedsheet. Some will come with a frame for easy mounting, but if yours is just the cloth itself, find yourself a washing line and some pegs and it will be just as good.

EDITING SOFTWARE If you have access to a desktop or laptop computer, then the chances are you have an editing suite already.

On a PC look for a programme called Windows Movie Maker, and on a Mac look for iMovie. These programmes are free, so if you don't have them you can download them for free from the Microsoft or Apple websites.

There are more sophisticated programs out there including Avid, Final Cut Pro and Premiere Pro, but these can be expensive so we recommend them only for advanced movie makers. You should find everything you need for these projects in the free software mentioned above, and other alternatives are available.

Each editing system varies and has its own tools. For specific instructions relating to the editing components within these projects, check within your programme or app for guidance on how to apply the steps.

INDEX

AUTHOR BIOGRAPHIES

Dan Farrell and Donna Bamford are the founding directors of Sparks Film and Media Arts, a film school for young people based in London. Since 2010, Sparks has worked with over 3000 young movie makers, using their unique and practical approach to produce more than 1000 movies. Sparks aims to deliver experiences where members not only have huge amounts of fun, but where they also have a say. Every child leaves with new skills and confidence, feeling inspired to try their very best.

Dan and Donna would like to thank Sheena Holliday, Simon Pollard, Sadie St. Hilaire, and Sarah Whitaker and all of the inspirational people who make up the Sparks team.

You can join the worldwide network of young movie makers by sharing your movies at www.sparks-ignite.com/tmmb.

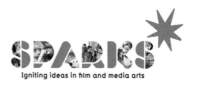

Igniting ideas in film and media arts